"*The Truth of the Cross* is the best book on the cross I have read. It is a 'must' for every church library and a book that I will give away many times to friends. This is so because it is sober (i.e., it contains historically informed reflections on salient biblical texts), sensible (i.e., it is well-argued), simple (i.e., it holds the reader's attention through grabbing illustrations and even a seventh-grader can get its substance), and spiritual (i.e., it comes from a heart set ablaze by the Spirit)."

—Dr. Bruce K. Waltke, Professor
Reformed Theological Seminary

"The cross stands at the very center of our Christian lives. Still, many Christians are confused about the heart of the gospel, for many deviant views are in the air. R. C. Sproul blows the fog away in this wonderfully clear, theologically profound, and pastorally rich work. Learn afresh or anew what God has accomplished in the cross, so that you will boast only in the cross of Jesus Christ."

—Dr. Thomas R. Schreiner, Professor
The Southern Baptist Theological Seminary

"The gospel is a message of good news that something extraordinary has happened. At the heart of that message is that Jesus, God the Son incarnate, has atoned for the sins of all His people, turning away the righteous wrath of God. The gospel is a cross-shaped message. Sadly, in our day, this message is being re-shaped into other forms, and the results are not happy. We can give thanks for this volume by R. C. Sproul, however, because in it he steps into the breach once more to provide a clear, concise, and thoughtful case for the biblical and historic Christian gospel of the cross."

—DR. R. SCOTT CLARK, ASSOCIATE PROFESSOR
Westminster Seminary California

THE TRUTH OF THE CROSS

THE TRUTH OF THE CROSS

R. C. SPROUL

ʀ

Reformation Trust

PUBLISHING

A DIVISION OF LIGONIER MINISTRIES · ORLANDO, FLORIDA

The Truth of the Cross

© Copyright 2007 by R. C. Sproul

Published by Reformation Trust Publishing
a division of Ligonier Ministries
400 Technology Park, Lake Mary, FL 32746
www.ligonier.org   www.reformationtrust.com

Third printing, July 2008
Printed in the United States of America

Cover design: Kirk DouPonce, www.DogEaredDesign.com
Interior design and typeset: Katherine Lloyd, Sisters, Ore.

All Scripture quotations, unless otherwise indicated, are taken from
the New King James Version®. Copyright © 1982 by Thomas Nelson.
Used by permission. All rights reserved.

Library of Congress Cataloging-in-Publication Data

    Sproul, R. C. (Robert Charles), 1939-
    The truth of the cross / R.C. Sproul.
      p. cm.
    ISBN 1-56769-087-4
    1. Jesus Christ--Crucifixion. I. Title.
    BT453.S663 2007
    232'.3--dc22

                    2007015926

To R. C. Sproul Jr. ("Precious"),
for his consistent and courageous
stand for biblical truth.

TABLE OF CONTENTS

One

THE NECESSITY OF
AN ATONEMENT

I 'm fascinated by the information that is put out by advertising agencies. It seems that the ad business keeps getting more and more sophisticated as agencies seek to position businesses and products in the marketplace. To that end, billions of dollars are spent every year to create what we call logos—little images, pictures, or symbols that instantly identify a brand or a product and communicate something about it, such as its history, its value, or its significance. I've heard it said that the most recognizable logo in the United

States of America is probably the Golden Arches that you find outside McDonald's restaurants.

The Christian faith also has a universal symbol—the cross. Why the cross? After all, Christianity has many aspects. We see these many facets in the field of systematic theology, which is divided into numerous subsections, such as theology proper, which is the study of God Himself; pneumatology, which is the study of the person and work of the Holy Spirit; ecclesiology, which is the study of the church; soteriology, which is the study of salvation; and so on.

But one of the most important subdivisions of theology is Christology, which is the study of the person and work of Christ. Within that field of study, when we want to get at the aspect that is most crucial, the aspect that we may call the "crux" of the matter of Jesus' person and work, we go immediately to the cross. The words *crucial* and *crux* both have their root in the Latin word for "cross," *crux*, and they have come into the English language with their current meanings because the concept of the cross is at the very center and core of biblical Christianity. In a very real sense, the cross crystallizes the essence of the ministry of Jesus.

This was the view of the apostle Paul. In his first letter to the church at Corinth, Paul made an astonishing statement about the importance of the cross to the entirety of the Christian faith: "And I, brethren, when I came to you, did not come with excellence of speech or of wisdom declaring to you the testimony of God. For I determined not to know anything among you except Jesus Christ and Him crucified" (1 Cor. 2:1–2). Paul was a man who had the equivalent of two Ph.D.s in theology by the time he was 21 years of age, a man who wrote with great insight on the whole scope of theology. Nevertheless, he said that the focal point of his teaching, preaching, and ministry among the Corinthians was simply "Jesus Christ and Him crucified."

When the apostle made that statement, he obviously was engaged in the literary art of hyperbole. The Greek prefix *hyper* is the source of our word *super*, and it indicates a degree of emphasis. *Hyper* takes a root word and makes it emphatic. In this case, the root word comes from the Greek verb "to throw." So hyperbole is literally a "super throwing"; it is a form of emphasis that uses intentional exaggeration. This is a common device in communication. Sometimes, when a child disobeys, a parent may say in exasperation, "I've told you ten thousand times not to do that." The parent doesn't mean literally ten thousand times, and no one who overhears the parent understands him or her to mean literally ten thousand times. Everybody understands that a statement like that is an exaggeration—an exaggeration born not out of deceitfulness or falsehood, but out of an intent to bring emphasis.

That's what Paul was doing when he told the Corinthians he had determined to know *nothing* except Christ crucified. Clearly Paul was determined to know all kinds of things besides the person and work of Jesus. He wanted to teach the Corinthians about the deep things of the character and nature of God the Father. He planned to instruct them about the person and work of the Holy Spirit, about Christian ethics, and about many other things that go beyond the immediate scope of Christ's work on the cross. So why, then, did he say this? The answer is obvious. Paul was saying that in all of his teaching, in all of his preaching, in all of his missionary activity, the central point of importance was the cross. In effect, this teacher was saying to his students, "You might forget other things that I teach you, but don't *ever* forget the cross, because it was on the cross, through the cross, and by the cross that our Savior performed His work of redemption and gathered His people for eternity."

In placing this emphasis on the cross, Paul was speaking for all of the New Testament writers. If we could read the New Testament with virgin eyes, as if we were the first generation of people to hear the message, I think it would be clear that the crucifixion was at the very core of the preaching, teaching, and catechizing of the New Testament community—along with, of course, the attending capstone of Christ's work, His resurrection and subsequent ascension. The significance, the purpose, and the meaning of the cross of Christ are unfolded to us in the New Testament.

If it is true that the cross is of central importance to biblical Christianity, it seems that it is essential for Christians to have some understanding of its meaning

in biblical terms. That would be true in any generation, but it's particularly necessary in this one. I doubt
there has been a period in the two thousand years of
Christian history when the significance, the centrality,
and even the *necessity* of the cross have been more con-
troversial than now. There have been other periods in
church history when theologies emerged that regarded
the cross of Christ as an unnecessary event, but never
before in Christian history has the need for an atonement been as widely challenged as it is today.

People tell me that they are not Christians, not
so much because they have never been convinced of
the truth claims of Christianity, but because they have
never been convinced of the need for what the Bible
teaches. How many times have you heard people say,
"That may be true, but I personally don't feel the need
for Jesus," or "I don't need the church," or "I don't need
Christianity"? When people say something like this to
me, I try to steer the conversation to the question of
the truth of Christianity. I believe that if we can con-
vince people of the truth of the identity of Christ and

the truth of the work He accomplished, it will become instantly apparent to them that they need it.

On one occasion, while I was waiting for my wife, Vesta, in a shopping mall, I noticed a bookstore and I stepped inside. There were counters and counters of books in that store, with the various categories marked prominently: fiction, nonfiction, business, sports, self-improvement, marriage, children's stories, and so on. In the very back of the store was the religion section, and it consisted of only four shelves, making it one of the smallest segments in the store. The material on those racks was not what would be called mainstream, orthodox, classical Christianity. I wondered, "Why does this store sell fiction and self-improvement, but place no premium on the content of biblical truth as part of its program?"

I realized the store wasn't there as a ministry. It was there for business, to make a profit. So I assumed the reason there were no solid Christian books was that there weren't a lot of people asking, "Where can I find a book that will teach me about the depths and the riches of the atonement of Christ?" Even when we go to a Christian bookstore, we find little evidence that people are seeking in-depth understanding of something as central as the atonement.

I thought about these things, and I came to the conclusion that people are not concerned about an atonement. They are basically convinced they have no need for it. They aren't asking: "How can I be reconciled to God? How can I escape the judgment of God?" If anything has been lost from our culture, it is the idea that human beings are privately, personally, individually, ultimately, inexorably accountable to God for their lives.

If everybody in the world woke up and said, "Someday I have to stand before my Maker and give an account for every word I've ever spoken, every deed I've ever done, every thought I've ever thought, and every task I've failed to do," several things could happen. They could say, "I'm accountable, but isn't it great that the One to Whom and before Whom I am accountable isn't concerned about the kind of life I lead, because He understands that boys will be boys and that girls will be girls." In that case, nothing would change. But if people understood that there is a holy God and that sin is an offense against that holy God, they would break down the doors of our churches and ask, "What must I do to be saved?"

I once went to the hospital with a kidney stone. It wasn't a life-threatening thing—it just seemed like it. I'm one of those people who, when in pain, will do everything in his power to deny that it's there so I won't have to see the doctor, have him probe around, and hear him tell me the bad news. But when I got this kidney stone, within two minutes I was on the telephone calling the doctor. When I got to the hospital, the doctors couldn't figure out what was wrong with me. As I waited for the tests to come back, lying flat on my back in pain, I flipped through the television channels and stopped at a religious broadcast, where a preacher was reading the Christmas story. In the course of things, he read the Annunciation: "For there is born to you this day in the city of David a Savior, who is Christ the Lord" (Luke 2:11). I can't tell you how many thousands of times I have read or heard that phrase, but when I was in that hospital bed with my future uncertain, it hit me like a sledgehammer. I said to myself, "That's exactly what I need—a Savior."

My point is this: I felt a need for a Savior because I was hurting. I was fearful, and matters of life and death were central in my attention. But that's not the way it is under normal circumstances in the day-to-day flow of people's lives. Our need for salvation is not a paramount concern. Christianity, however, operates on the primary assumption that man is in need of salvation.

The prevailing doctrine of justification today is not justification by faith alone. It's not even justification by good works or by a combination of faith and works. The prevailing notion of justification in Western culture today is justification by death. It's assumed that all one has to do to be received into the everlasting arms of God is to die.

In some instances, the prevailing indifference to the cross mutates into outright hostility. I once was asked to deliver a lecture explaining the relationship between the old and new covenants. In the course of delivering this lecture, I referred to Christ's death as a substitutionary, vicarious sacrifice for the sins of others. To my surprise, someone in the back of the room yelled out, "That's primitive and obscene." I was taken aback for a moment, so I asked, "What did you say?" He said it again with great hostility: "That's primitive and obscene." At that point, I had recovered from my surprise, and I told the man I actually liked his choice of adjectives. It is primitive for a blood sacrifice to be made to satisfy the justice of a transcendent and holy God, but sin is a primitive thing that is basic to our human existence, so God chose to communicate His love, mercy, and redemption to us through this primitive work. And the cross is an obscenity, because all of the corporate sin of God's people was laid on Christ. The cross was the ugliest, most obscene thing in the history of the world. So I thanked the man for his observation. But my point is that the man was extremely hostile to the whole idea of the atonement.

Of course, this widespread doubt about the need for an atonement did not appear overnight. In fact, the atonement has long been the subject of debate within the church.

I have a theologian friend who frequently makes this statement: "In church history, there are basically only three types of theology." Although there have been many schools with numerous names and various subtle nuances, generically there are only three kinds of theology historically—what we call Augustinianism, Semi-Pelagianism, and Pelagianism. In basic terms, Augustinianism holds that salvation rests on God's grace alone; Semi-Pelagianism teaches that salvation rests on human cooperation with God's grace; and Pelagianism believes that salvation can be achieved without God's grace. Virtually every church in history has fallen into one of those three categories.

Augustinianism and Semi-Pelagianism, in my opinion, represent significant debates within the Christian family, differences of opinion about biblical interpretation and theology among Christians. However, Pelagianism in its various forms is not an intramural issue among Christians, but is at best sub-Christian and at worst anti-Christian. I say that because of Pelagianism's view of the necessity of the cross.

Just as there are three basic types of theology,

there are three basic views of the atonement with respect to its necessity historically. First, there are those who believe that an atonement is *absolutely unnecessary.* The Pelagians in all their forms fall into this category. Pelagianism, originating in the fourth century; Socinianism, which arose in the sixteenth and seventeenth centuries; and what we would call liberalism as a distinctive theology today are all essentially non-Christian because at the heart of each is a denial of the atonement of Jesus Christ. These schools of thought, by taking away the reconciling action of Christ from the New Testament, are left with nothing but moralisms. For them, the cross is where Jesus died as a moral example for men. They view Him as an existential hero, as One Who brings inspiration to us by His commitment and devotion to self-sacrifice and to His humanistic concerns. But these moralisms are anything but unique and hardly worthy of allegiance. In Pelagianism, there is no salvation, no Savior, and no atonement because in Pelagianism no such salvation is *necessary.*

Second, there are those who believe an atonement

is only *hypothetically necessary*. This view historically expresses the idea that God could have redeemed us by a host of ways and means, or He could have chosen to overlook human sin. However, He did something dramatic when He committed Himself to a certain course of action. He chose to redeem us by the cross, by an atonement. Once He committed Himself, it became necessary, not *de jure* or *de facto*, but *de pacto*—that is, by virtue of a pact or a covenant that God made by issuing a promise that He would do a particular thing. The promise was gratuitous in that it was not necessary for Him to do it, but He nevertheless made the promise. He was then committed to that course of action. That's what is meant by a hypothetical necessity for an atonement.

The third view, which is the classical, orthodox Christian view, which I am convinced is the biblical view, is that an atonement was not merely hypothetically necessary for man's redemption, but was *absolutely necessary* if any person was ever going to be reconciled to God and redeemed. For this reason, orthodoxy has held for centuries that the cross is an essential of Christianity, essential in the sense that it is a sine qua non, "without which it could not be." If you take away the cross as an atoning act, you take away Christianity.

The statement that the cross was an absolutely necessary prerequisite for redemption immediately raises the "Why?" question. The answer lies, as it has even since the time of Augustine and Pelagius, with our understanding of the nature of the character of God and the nature of sin. If we are defective in understanding the character of God or understanding the nature of sin, it is inevitable that we will come to the conclusion that an atonement was not necessary. Therefore, we will spend the next few chapters wrestling with these crucial issues.

Two

THE JUST GOD

Thehere are certain theologians who stand out as giants as we survey the course of church history— men such as Augustine of Hippo, Thomas Aquinas, Martin Luther, John Calvin, and Jonathan Edwards. Normally we would say that Augustine was the greatest theologian of the first millennium of church history. We are familiar with the great men of the Reformation period and later, such as Luther, Calvin, and Edwards. But when it comes to the intervening era, the Middle Ages, we hear of few great thinkers other than Aquinas. Yet there was a theologian-philosopher from that period who made an enormous contribution to church history—Anselm of Canterbury.

Anselm left a legacy of three very important works, all of which were brief. The first two were works in apologetics. One is called the *Monologion* and the other is the *Proslogion*. It was in this latter book that Anselm gave his famous ontological argument for the existence of God. Perhaps his greatest contribution was his little work that appeared under the Latin title *Cur Deus Homo*? This title literally means "Why the God-man?" In other words, Anselm was asking why there was an incarnation. Why did Christ become a man?

At the heart of Anselm's answer to that question was his understanding of the character of God. Anselm saw that the chief reason a God-man was necessary was the justice of God. That may seem to be a strange answer. Thinking of the cross and of Christ's atonement, we assume that the thing that most strenuously motivated God to send Christ into the world was His love or His mercy. As a result, we tend to overlook the characteristic of God's nature that makes the atonement absolutely necessary—His justice.

God is loving, but a major part of what He loves is His own perfect character, with a major aspect being the importance of maintaining justice and righteousness. Though God pardons sinners and makes great provision for expressing His mercy, He will never negotiate His justice. If we fail to understand that, the cross of Christ will be utterly meaningless to us.

What do we mean when we speak of God's justice? In the ancient Jewish mind, justice was never abstract. That's why, in the Old Testament, justice inevitably was linked with the concept of righteousness. Righteousness means doing what is right. Therefore, God's justice has to do with His internal righteousness, His character, which defines everything He does. God never acts according to injustice. He never violates any of the standards or canons of righteousness. A simple definition of God's justice is "His eternal, immutable commitment always to do what is right."

Genesis 18 contains a narrative that is both fascinating and instructive. This is the story of the intercession of the patriarch Abraham on behalf of the inhabitants of Sodom and Gomorrah. These cities were so evil in Old Testament times that they became literary symbols for corruption. Just to say the names *Sodom* and *Gomorrah* conjures up ghastly imagery of corrupt and decadent cities. Yet Abraham dared ask God to spare these cities, and his interaction with God has much to teach us about God's justice.

The narrative begins in Genesis 18:16:

> Then the men rose from there and looked toward Sodom, and Abraham went with them to send them on the way. And the LORD said, "Shall I hide from Abraham what I am doing, since Abraham shall surely become a great and mighty nation, and all of the nations of the earth shall be blessed in him? For I have known him, in order that he may command his children and his household after him, that they keep the way of the LORD, to do righteousness and justice, that the LORD may bring to Abraham what He has spoken to him."

God appears to be musing in this narrative, asking Himself whether He ought to let Abraham know what He is planning or keep it from him. Yet He's obviously about to tell Abraham what He's going to do, because God has assured Abraham that he will be the father of a great nation and has made His covenant promise to Abraham and to his descendants. God has a destiny for His people, Abraham's descendants, which destiny is defined here in the text by the terms *righteousness* and *justice*. God has not selected Abraham capriciously out of all the pagans of the world. On the contrary, He's creating a nation that is to be holy, to be set apart, a people who will bear witness to the character of God by imitating Him in the pursuit of righteousness and of justice.

Therefore, beginning in verse 20, we hear the announcement that God has for Abraham:

And the LORD said, "Because the outcry against Sodom and Gomorrah is great, and because their sin is very grave, I will go down

now and see whether they have done altogether according to the outcry against it that
has come to Me; and if not, I will know." Then
the men turned away from there and went
toward Sodom, but Abraham still stood before
the LORD. And Abraham came near and said,
"Would You also destroy the righteous with
the wicked?"

There is drama in this passage. God says: "I'm
going to visit Sodom and Gomorrah because I have
heard a great outcry about the severity of their wick-
edness and the gravity of their evil." That means He
is going to visit the cities *with judgment*. God already
knows what's going on there because He is omniscient;
He has no need to perform an eyewitness investiga-
tion in order to learn the truth about this matter.

Abraham clearly understands that God's intention
is judgment, for he comes to God with a theological question. Abraham is indeed the father of the
faithful—he's the venerable patriarch of the Old Testament, a man after God's own heart, one who is the

spokesman for goodness, justice, and truth. Therefore, we would think that Abraham would be a better theologian than he indicates by the question that he brings before God. Never would we expect Abraham, in his elevated status as the patriarch of the Old Testament, to ask the Deity a question that is a thinly veiled form of blasphemy.

However, Abraham does just that. He asks: "Would You . . . destroy the righteous with the wicked?" In other words, Abraham is asking, "God, when you bring Your judgment on Sodom and Gomorrah, will You destroy both the innocent and the guilty?" To ask a question like that is to answer it with respect to God.

As a child, I wasn't yet a Christian, but I had some ideals. Among these was the American dream of truth and justice for everyone, and I hated injustice. On one occasion when I was in grade school, one of my friends, David King, lit a cherry bomb in the classroom when the teacher had her back turned to the class. When it blew up, it sounded like an atomic bomb. The teacher jumped in the air, dropped the chalk, and turned around horror-stricken. Immediately she asked, "All right, who did it?" Not everybody in the class knew who did it, but the vast majority of us could guess who the guilty party was. The teacher had a good idea, too, because David had a reputation for these kinds of pranks. I sat in the back of the room right next to David, and I knew that he had done it. But there was a code—you didn't "rat" on your friends. Because of that, when the teacher asked who had lit the cherry bomb, nobody confessed. She made the entire class stay after school until somebody confessed or turned in the real culprit. That bothered me. The punishment she gave was an effective device for pedagogy and discipline, but it bothered me because it was not just. In order to get to the guilty party, our teacher punished the innocent people who didn't know who did the crime and who were not in on the crime. They were forced to stay after school, losing their freedom because of the teacher's strategy. What the teacher did may have been effective and it may have been practical, but it wasn't just.

God is not a frustrated schoolteacher. God is omniscient; He doesn't have to play games to ferret out the guilty party. He is just and righteous, so

He would never, ever punish the innocent. Abraham should have known that. The question he asked God was an insult to the Deity.

Abraham then begins to negotiate and bargain with God. Beginning in Genesis 18:24, he says:

"Suppose there were fifty righteous within the city; would You also destroy the place and not spare it for the fifty righteous that were in it? Far be it from You to do such a thing as this, to slay the righteous with the wicked, so that the righteous should be as the wicked; far be it from You! Shall not the Judge of all the earth do right?"

Now my faith in Abraham is restored. After asking such a ridiculous question—"Would You . . . destroy the righteous with the wicked?"—Abraham now speaks correctly. He says, "Far be it from You to do such a thing as this, to slay the righteous with the wicked." Now his theology is sound, though I still have to wonder whether Abraham fully grasped how far it would be from God to do such an unjust thing. By his rhetorical question, "Shall not the Judge of all of the earth do right?" Abraham shows that he sees how manifestly obvious it is that the Judge of all of the earth *will* do what is right, simply because that's all the Judge of the earth knows how to do.

God then confirms Abraham's belief when He assures the patriarch that in His mercy and in His kindness, He is willing to spare the whole city if fifty righteous people are to be found there. God says: "I'll even be merciful to the guilty. So far am I from punishing the innocent, I'll actually let the guilty go in order to protect the innocent."

In the mid-1990s, there was consuming interest in the United States over the murder trial of O. J. Simpson. People grew angrier as the trial stretched on. Many people were convinced he was obviously guilty and ought to be locked up. But that trial, perhaps more than any other, pointed out a principle of the U.S. criminal justice system that places the burden of proof squarely on the prosecution, requiring that charges be proved beyond "a reasonable doubt" so as to protect the innocent. In the American justice system, we recognize that since we're not infallible and not omniscient, we don't always know for sure who has committed a crime. If we're going to err, the system says, let us err on the side of clemency rather than on the side of severity.

But Abraham is not satisfied with God's promise to grant clemency to all for the sake of fifty righteous ones. In verse 27, he continues, saying:

Then Abraham answered and said, "Indeed now, I who am but dust and ashes have taken it upon myself to speak to the Lord: Suppose there were five less than the fifty righteous; would You destroy all of the city for lack of five?" So He said, "If I find there forty-five, I will not destroy it." And he spoke to Him yet again and said, "Suppose there should be forty found there." So He said, "I will not do it for the sake of forty." Then he said, "Let not the Lord be angry, and I will speak: Suppose thirty should be found there?" So He said, "I will not do it if I find thirty there." And he said, "Indeed now, I have taken it upon myself to speak to the Lord: Suppose twenty should be found there?" So he said, "I will not destroy it for the sake of twenty." Then he said, "Let not the Lord be angry. And I will speak but once more: Suppose ten should be found there?" And He said, "I will not destroy it for the sake of ten." So the LORD went His way as soon as He had finished speaking with Abraham, and Abraham returned to his place.

The Bible tells us that God couldn't find ten righteous people among all the inhabitants of these cities. As a result, God's judgment fell. It fell not because God is cruel, harsh, or lacking in love. It happened because God is just and righteous.

By all rights, this judgment would be the fate of the entire human race. Not only were there not ten righteous in Sodom, there are not ten in all the world. Romans 3:10b tells us, "There is none righteous, no, not one." All men have offended God's justice and deserve His judgment.

Thus, the necessity for the atonement of Christ finds its genesis, in the first instance, in the character of God. Because He is holy and righteous, He cannot excuse sin. Rather, He must pass judgment on it. The Judge of all the earth must do right. Therefore, He must punish sinners—or provide a way to atone for their sin.

Three

DEBTORS, ENEMIES, AND CRIMINALS

A few years ago, I received a complimentary copy of a newly published collection of quotations, much like *Bartlett's Familiar Quotations*. Although I was pleased to receive it, I had no idea why it had been sent until, leafing through the pages of quotations from Immanuel Kant, John Stuart Mill, Aristotle, Plato, Thomas Aquinas, and Augustine, to my utter astonishment, I came upon a quotation from me. The editors had graced me by including a statement I had made. I had never thought that the statement was particularly significant. However, someone thought it was significant enough to merit inclusion in the book. The quotation was: "Sin is cosmic treason."

With those words, I was trying to communicate the seriousness of human sin. We rarely take the time to think through the ramifications of our sin. We fail to realize that in even the slightest sins we commit, such as little white lies and other peccadilloes, we are violating the law of the Creator of the universe. In the smallest sin we defy God's right to rule and to reign over His creation. Instead, we seek to usurp for ourselves the authority and the power that belong properly to God. Even the slightest sin does violence to His holiness, to His glory, and to His righteousness. Every sin, no matter how seemingly insignificant, is truly an act of treason against the cosmic King.

There are two aspects of the one problem we must understand if we are to grasp the necessity of the atonement of Christ. In the previous chapter, we saw one aspect—that God is just. In other words, He cannot tolerate unrighteousness. He must do what is right. But I also alluded to the other aspect of the problem—we have violated God's justice and earned His displeasure.

We are cosmic traitors. We must recognize this problem within ourselves if we are to grasp the necessity of the cross.

"Cosmic treason" is one possible characterization of sin, but the Bible has several other meaningful descriptions that shed light on the need for the cross and on what Christ accomplished there. In fact, there are three distinct ways in which human sin is described and communicated biblically—it is called a debt, it is called a state of enmity, and it is called a crime. With these descriptions, the Bible helps us see our sin for the terrible thing it is.

First, sin is characterized as *a debt*. We see this depiction of sin most clearly in the prayer Jesus taught His disciples, wherein He instructed them to ask, "'And forgive us our debts, as we forgive our debtors'" (Matt. 6:12). He later taught in the parable of the unforgiving servant that Christians have an obligation to forgive others' debts because of God's forgiveness of their own debts (Matt. 18:21–35).

In order to understand the full implications of what Scripture is saying when it tells us that man incurs a debt by his sin, we have to understand the role of God as the Sovereign Lord over the universe. When we speak of God's sovereignty, we are discussing His authority. The word *authority* has another word in it—*author*. Because God is the Author of all things, He has authority over all that He has created.

Perhaps I'm laboring the obvious here, but I notice that in our culture there's much confusion over the nature of authority. When we talk about duly constituted authority, we're talking about a person or office that has the right to impose obligation. If I am under someone's authority, that person has the right to impose obligations on me, so if he or she issues a morally sound command to me, I am responsible to carry out that obligation. Likewise, we are under God's authority by virtue of His authorship of all things, so He has the intrinsic and absolute right to impose obligations on us. When He does so, we "owe" obedience to Him. If we fail to perform the obligations He places on us, we incur a debt. So according to this understanding of sin, God is the Creditor and we are the debtors.

It's one thing to be in debt and to be on a debt-retirement program, whereby we pay off what we owe a little bit at a time. But the indebtedness that we have with respect to obedience to God is impossible for us to pay back on any installment plan. Why? To answer that question, we must understand the true nature of the obligation God imposes on His creatures. How righteous are we required to be? How moral are we called to be? God demands perfect obedience, sinless perfection.

This is the crux of the problem. If I am responsible to be perfect, and I sin once, what must I do to be perfect? How much interest must I pay in addition to the principal in order to make up for the blemish? What do I have to do to become perfect after I have once been imperfect? Simply put, it is impossible. Once we sin, we become like Lady Macbeth, who, after she manipulated her husband to commit murder, could not wipe out that indelible spot. Likewise, we cannot expunge our sin debt.

We try to get around the helplessness of this situation in modern culture by declaring that everybody deserves a second chance. My response is, "Who says so?" Does justice require that everybody get a second chance? A second chance is grace. It is mercy. Grace and mercy are *never* deserved. So it is nonsense to say that everyone deserves a second chance. But even if that nonsensical, hypothetical condition were true, what good would it do us? How long ago did we use up our second chance?

Our problem is not that we are almost impeccable moral creatures with tiny blemishes marring an otherwise perfect record. Rather, the Scriptures describe us as woefully inadequate in terms of our obedience to God. It's not that we're just tainted by a peccadillo now and then. We have incurred a debt that's impossible for us to pay.

If somebody said, "R. C., you owe $10,000, so we'll set up a program by which you can pay off your debts," I could handle that. But what would I do if I were told, "You owe $10 billion and you've got three days to pay it"? Would it be possible for me to pay it? It's possible, but it's far more likely that I would fail to find the money. In the case of my indebtedness to God, however, there's no possibility at all that I will be able to pay what I owe. There is no way any of us can pay that debt.

Second, sin is regarded from the biblical perspective as an expression of *enmity*. In other words, sin can be seen as a violation of the personal relationship human beings are supposed to have with their Creator. By sinning, we communicate not love, affection, or devotion to our Creator. Instead, we reject Him and declare our hostility toward Him.

It is important that we understand that God manifests no enmity toward us. He has never broken a promise. He has never violated a covenant. He has never sworn a vow to us that He failed to pay. He has never treated a human being in this world unjustly. He has never violated us as creatures. In short, He has kept His side of the relationship perfectly. But we have violated Him. We are the ones who violate the creature-Creator relationship. By our sin, we show ourselves to be God's enemies. Therefore, with respect to enmity, He is the injured party, the violated One.

Now, people may say: "That's simple. We learned that in Sunday school." But I find people every day who are deeply angry against God because they feel He somehow has not given them a fair deal. "How could God allow this to happen to me?" is the complaint. The unspoken statement there is, "If God were really good, if God were really just, He would recognize my merit and treat me accordingly. He would give me more than I have. God's not fair." This feeling that God has somehow injured us is deeply lodged in our bones.

Injustice abounds in this world between people. One person lies to another, cheats another, or harms another. On the horizontal plane, there's much injustice. But how much injustice goes vertically from God to man? If someone violates me and makes me a victim of his unjust activity, I can say to God, "O God, avenge me of this, vindicate me, restore me, redeem me from this man's unjust activity toward me." But is it legitimate to say, "God, the fact that You allowed him to commit an injustice to me is unjust on Your part"? No. Nothing could ever happen to me in this world that would give me a just reason to assault the integrity of God in terms of our relationship. He is the injured party, not we.

According to the Scriptures, we have acted in such a way as to rupture our relationship with God. We exercise and manifest our enmity by our continual disobedience. He is sorely displeased with our offenses. He is angry with our sin. As a result, there is estrangement between man and God.

Third, sin is characterized in the Bible as a *crime*. In the classical Presbyterian tradition, we have a definition of sin. The Westminster Shorter Catechism, Question No. 14, asks, "What is sin?" It then gives this answer: "Sin is any want of conformity to, or transgression of, the law of God." The words *want of conformity to* and *transgression of* indicate a failure to keep the Law of God. So in this sense, sin is a crime.

As we saw earlier when we considered sin as a debt, we have a duty to obey God because He has authority over us by virtue of having created us. That authority gives Him the right to impose obligations on us. He does so by way of the demands that He makes in terms of our obedience. God does not rule by referendum or by plebiscite. Neither does He give suggestions or recommendations. He gives commandments—"Thou shalt . . ." or "Thou shalt not . . ."—which we call apodictic law flowing from His absolute authority and sovereignty.

When God issues a law, when He legislates a kind of behavior, it is our duty as His creatures to do as He says. A moral obligation to conform to that law is imposed on us justly from His hand. When we don't conform, we are breaking that law, which means we are committing a crime in the sight of God. When a crime is committed, His justice has been violated and we are worthy of sanctions.

According to this understanding of sin, God functions as the Judge. When we fail to meet our obligations, God has an obligation to bring judgment on us. As Abraham recognized, the Judge of all the earth must do right. A just judge, a good judge, is not one who lets a crime go unpunished. God is supremely a God of law and order. God not only enacts laws, He enforces His laws. Therefore, if we commit even the slightest sin, we're in trouble. God is just, and His justice demands that sin be punished.

In the previous chapter, I noted that Anselm stressed the point that the justice and righteousness of God constituted the primary need for the cross. According to Anselm, each of the three characterizations of sin that we have considered—a debt, a state of enmity, and a crime—constitutes a violation of that divine righteousness, which necessitates satisfaction. When we incur a debt by failing to meet an obligation before God, that debt must be satisfied—that is, the requirements must be met in a satisfactory way. When sin creates enmity and estrangement, the requirements to end that estrangement and bring about reconciliation must be satisfied. When we commit a crime against God, His justice must be satisfied—a payment or penalty must be given or made that satisfies the demands of divine justice, or it will be compromised. We see that at the heart of Anselm's understanding of the atonement is this concept of satisfaction.

How is such satisfaction to be achieved? It is accomplished by the other actor in the drama of the atonement—the Lord Jesus Christ. For each characterization of sin in the Bible, Jesus plays a crucial role. We may summarize the roles of each of the actors in this way:

Sin as . . .	Man	God	Christ
Debt	Debtor	Creditor	Surety
Enmity	Enemy	Violated One	Mediator
Crime	Criminal	Judge	Substitute

When sin is depicted as a debt, the New Testament calls Christ our Surety (Heb. 7:22). That's an economic term, just as *debt* is an economic term. With this language, the Bible tells us that Christ is the One Who cosigns the note. He is the One Who stands there, backing up our indebtedness, taking on Himself the requirement of what must be paid.

With respect to the characterization of sin as an expression of enmity, the role Christ plays is that of a Mediator. In human conflicts, the mediator stands in the middle in order to bring the two opposing parties together. We call that reconciliation, and that is exactly what Christ does. He reconciles God to man. As the apostle Paul writes, "God was in Christ reconciling the world to Himself" (2 Cor. 5:19a).

When sin is characterized as a crime, we see that Christ is the One Who actually comes under judgment in the drama of the atonement. He functions as the Substitute, the One Who stands in the place of the true criminals—you and me.

Christ, then, is the One Who made satisfaction. By His work on the cross, He satisfied the demands of God's justice with regard to our debt, our state of enmity, and our crime. In light of the facts of God's justice and our sinfulness, it is not difficult to see the absolute necessity of the atonement.

We must be careful that we understand exactly how Jesus functions in this crucial role. It is common to encounter grave distortions of the biblical concept of the atonement. For instance, according to one popular view, God the Father is enraged at man, but God the Son identifies so closely with our fallenness that, in essence, He sides with us in our need and acts as our Mediator to calm the Father's anger. The Father is about to punish everybody and send them to hell, but the Son says: "Punish Me instead. Let Me stand in their place. Let Me not only mediate the discussion, but let Me absorb the anger. You can heap Your wrath on Me." According to this view, there is a tension or a split within the Godhead itself, as if the Father has an agenda and the Son persuades Him to change His mind.

This may sound like a ridiculous scenario, but it is a serious objection raised at a technical level by sophisticated theologians. It's also a widespread, prevalent belief among Christians, perhaps because the Son seems more loving, patient, and compassionate than the Father. In this sense, evangelical Christians tend to be Unitarians of the second person of the Trinity. There's much warm affection for Jesus, but the Father is almost totally ignored in Christian study, devotion, and liturgy.

Let me paint the biblical picture by use of the following scenario. Imagine that I go to a friend and say: "Don, I'm in trouble. I need to borrow $10,000. Would you lend me $10,000?" And Don says, "Sure." He lends me $10,000 and I understand that I now owe him $10,000. We have a perfectly legal, perfectly ethical arrangement. Unfortunately, I wake up one morning and I find out I can't pay the $10,000. Now I'm in big trouble. However, my sister says: "Don't worry about it. I'll pay the $10,000." So she pays Don the $10,000 that I owe. Now I owe Don nothing. My debt has been canceled 100 percent. In fact, he must receive that $10,000 legal tender in payment for the debt because the only responsibility I have to him is to pay the money. That's the way a debt is.

But suppose I were to break into Don's house and steal $10,000. Don comes home, finds his $10,000 missing, and calls the police. The police find my fingerprints, track me down, and find the $10,000 in my possession, so they arrest me. I might say: "I'm sorry that happened. Here, take the money. Give it back to Don and let's just forget it." Or perhaps I've spent the money by the time they arrest me, but my sister steps in again and says, "Wait a minute, I'll give him the $10,000." In either scenario, Don is not bound to receive that $10,000 and wipe the slate clean because not only have I incurred a "debt" to Don, I have committed a crime against him and have violated him as a person. He has the right to decide whether he will accept that payment and refuse to press charges—because he is the one who has been wronged.

When Jesus offers to make satisfaction for me, in order for that payment to be accepted, God the Father, Who is my Creditor, the party I have violated, and my Judge, must decide and decree that He will accept that payment from another in my behalf. In other words, if I owe God the death penalty because I sinned against Him, and Jesus says, "I will die for him," and then lays down His life and dies for me, would the Father be under any obligation whatsoever to accept that payment? No. There first must be a judgment by the Governor of the universe that He will in fact accept a substitutionary payment for my debt, my enmity, and my crime.

As we know, God did accept Jesus' substitutionary payment for us, so we see that there was a prior decision of the Father that was based on sheer grace. At some point before time began, He made the decision to accept the satisfaction made by a Substitute. We may think the Son is more loving than the Father, but Whose idea was it for us to have a Mediator? Who then sent the Mediator? As the Scriptures declare, "God so loved the world that He gave His only begotten Son . . ." (John 3:16a). God the Father, the One we violated by our sin, sent the Son to be the Mediator Who would reconcile us to Himself.

In this day, theologians tend to repudiate Anselm's insight and somehow think less of a God Who requires satisfaction. In many ways, they reject the whole idea of satisfaction. But we cannot read a page of the New Testament that does not drive us back to this concept. As Paul says in Romans when he's expounding the doctrine of justification, God set out "to demonstrate at the present time His righteousness, that He might be just and the justifier of the one who has faith in Jesus" (Rom. 3:26). That's what the cross is about—it displays the justice of God and the mercy of God. It is by virtue of the atonement that God can maintain His justice and yet demonstrate His mercy by providing satisfaction for those debtors who can't pay their debts, those enemies who can't find reconciliation to overcome their estrangement, and those criminals who can't pay for their crimes.

God says: "Justice will be done. The debt will be paid in full. The crime will be punished." He does not negotiate His justice at all. The fact that my debt is paid, the demands of reconciliation are met, and the punishment for my crime is given to my Substitute shows that in the cross we see perfect justice with perfect mercy. In the substitution that took place at the cross, we see the glorious grace of God—the very heartbeat of the Christian faith.

Four

RANSOMED
FROM ABOVE

There must have been times in Jesus' life, particularly toward the close of His earthly ministry, when, touching His human nature, He was frustrated. For instance, when He made His last trip from Galilee up to Jerusalem, He constantly focused attention on His coming hour, preparing His disciples for the fact that He was going to Jerusalem to die. But somehow it didn't get across to them.

Here's how the Gospel of Mark relates one of the incidents during that journey:

Now they were on the road, going up to Jerusalem, and Jesus was going before them; and they were amazed. And as they followed they were afraid. Then He took the twelve aside again and began to tell them the things that would happen to Him: "Behold, we are going up to Jerusalem, and the Son of Man will be betrayed to the chief priests and to the scribes; and they will condemn Him to death and deliver Him to the Gentiles; and they will mock Him, and scourge Him, and spit on Him, and kill Him. And the third day he will rise again." (Mark 10:32–34)

That was an extremely sobering warning. But after Jesus spoke those words, James and John appeared, asking Jesus to let them sit on His right and left in glory. This was a variation, of sorts, on the disciples' ongoing argument about which of them was the greatest. As Christ was preparing to enter into His grand passion, His closest friends were arguing about the inheritance.

It was in that context that Jesus said something

that is significant for our understanding of the atonement. He said:

> "You know that those who are considered rulers over the Gentiles lord it over them, and their great ones exercise authority over them. Yet it shall not be so among you; but whoever desires to become great among you shall be your servant. And whoever of you desires to be first shall be slave of all. For even the Son of Man did not come to be served, but to serve, and to give His life a ransom for many." (Mark 10:42b–45)

In His apparent frustration, Jesus was trying here to communicate to His disciples what His ministry was about. He was striving to state it succinctly and graphically so that His dull-witted disciples would understand once and for all what He was going to do. He said that He had not come that others might serve Him but that He might serve others by giving His life as a *ransom*.

The Greek word Mark uses here is interesting. In studying Greek, the first Greek verb a person usually learns is *luo*, which means "to loose, to set free, to unbind." *Luo* is the root of *lutron*, which Mark employs in this passage. "Ransom" is a good translation of *lutron* because a ransom has to do with loosing something, with setting free something that is held in captivity.

When we think of a ransom, we tend to think of kidnapping. In that context, the ransom is a monetary payment that a person demands in exchange for the release of someone taken captive. The idea of a ransom had that same connotation in the ancient world, but a ransom also could be a price that was paid to release a slave from bondage or to set free hostages who were being held in military conflicts.

While we do not see the word *ransom* used frequently in Scripture, the concept of a ransom stands behind the broad biblical term *redemption*. In biblical categories, a redeemer is one who takes action to set another free. Thus, God is said to be Israel's Redeemer when He delivers His people from bondage in Egypt. The exodus story is about redemption.

That brings us back to the cross, where Jesus made atonement for His people, satisfying the requirements of God's justice. As we have seen, the atonement is a multifaceted event—Jesus is shown providing surety for our debt to God, mediating the enmity between us and God, and offering Himself as a substitute to suffer God's judgment in our place. But He is also seen in the New Testament as the Redeemer, the One Who redeems His people from captivity, setting them free by offering Himself as a ransom.

This task was at the very heart of Jesus' mission. We remember that at the beginning of His ministry, Jesus went into the synagogue in His hometown of Nazareth and read the text of Isaiah 61:1–2, saying,

> "The Spirit of the LORD is upon Me,
> Because He has anointed Me
> To preach the gospel to the poor;
> He has sent me to heal the brokenhearted,
> To proclaim liberty to the captives
> And recovery of sight to the blind,
> To set at liberty those who are oppressed;

To proclaim the acceptable year of the Lord."
(Luke 4:18–19)

This prophecy set forth the character of the ministry of the Messiah, which was to include the release of captives. In other words, Jesus was saying He had come to set at liberty those who were in bondage. He would do it by paying a ransom.

We must be careful here. One of the views of the atonement that has competed for acceptance throughout church history is known as "the ransom theory," but this theory has been articulated in two different and often conflicting ways. The first holds that in the transaction on the cross, Jesus paid a ransom to Satan because Satan held fallen man under bondage. In other words, Satan was the kidnapper who had snatched us away from our Father's house, and Christ came and paid a ransom to the Devil to set us free.

It's easy to see how this theory could develop. After all, who usually sets a ransom? It is not established by some board of trade that comes in and figures out the going market rate. The price tag for the ransom

is set initially by the kidnapper, the slaveholder, or
the hostage taker. He determines the ransom price,
and then it's up to those who are trying to free the
kidnapped person, the slave, or the prisoner of war to
decide whether they attach enough value to the captive to justify the ransom. Because the New Testament
speaks of fallen man being in bondage to sin, and
because Satan is the enemy of God and the tempter, it
is easy to jump to the conclusion that Satan held us in
bondage and demanded a ransom from God.

The Bible clearly calls attention to the *Christus
Victor* element of the atonement, which is that aspect
of Christ's work by which He achieved a cosmic victory over powers and principalities, conquering the
Devil and ending his power over us. We see the conflict between Jesus and Satan from the very beginning
of Jesus' ministry, when the Spirit led Him into the
wilderness to be tempted by the Devil. Jesus withstood
that temptation, but Luke tells us that when it was
over the Devil departed from Him "until an oppor-
tune time" (Luke 4:13b). Satan went into retreat, but
not a permanent retreat. It was what we would call

a strategic withdrawal so that he could find a better place to launch another assault against Christ. This was a conflict that went on throughout the ministry of Jesus.

But Christ gained the victory over Satan at the cross. It happened just as God had declared it would in the earliest days of the human race. After Adam and Eve sinned, God came to them and pronounced curses on them, then turned to the Serpent and said, "'I will put enmity between you and the woman, and between your seed and her Seed; He shall bruise your head, and you shall bruise His heel'" (Gen. 3:15). This was the *proto-evangelium*, the first gospel ever preached. The New Testament writers would interpret these words as finding fulfillment in Christ's death, for on the cross Christ crushed the head of Satan, though in the process He suffered pain Himself, even the pain of death. But He was raised from the grave through the power of God, gaining absolute victory. "Having disarmed principalities and powers, He made a public spectacle of them, triumphing over them in it" (Col. 2:15).

However, the truth of the struggle between Christ and the Devil does not mean that the ransom of which Christ spoke was paid to Satan. Think of it for a moment. If Christ paid a ransom to Satan to deliver us from Satan's clutches, who is the victor? The kidnapper usually does not want permanent possession of his victim; rather, he wants the ransom he can get in exchange for his hostage's release. If he can get the ransom, he wins. So if the ransom was paid to Satan, the Devil laughed all the way to the bank and there is no *Christus Victor*. It must be *Satanus Victor*.

I favor the other expression of the ransom theory, which holds that the ransom was paid not to Satan but to God, because God was the One Who had to be satisfied. When the Bible speaks of ransom, it speaks of that ransom being paid not to a criminal but to the One Who is owed the price for redemption, the One Who is the offended party in the whole complex of sin—the Father. Jesus didn't negotiate with Satan for our salvation. Instead, He offered Himself in payment to the Father for us. By so offering Himself, He made redemption for His people, redeeming them from captivity.

The motif of ransom and redemption is an idea that is often overlooked, but it is deeply rooted in Scripture. To get a grasp on it, let's direct our attention to some rather obscure passages in the Bible that we may find strange. In the first of these, Exodus 21:1–6, God commands Moses to instruct the people of Israel as follows:

"Now these are the judgments which you shall set before them: If you buy a Hebrew servant, he shall serve six years; and in the seventh he shall go out free and pay nothing. If he comes in by himself, he shall go out by himself; if he comes in married, then his wife shall go out with him. If his master has given him a wife, and she has borne him sons or daughters, the wife and her children shall be her master's, and he shall go out by himself. But if the servant plainly says, 'I love my master, my wife, and my children; I will not go out free,' then his master shall bring him to the judges. He shall also bring him to the door, or to the doorpost,

and his master shall pierce his ear with an awl;
and he shall serve him forever."

What is the Bible saying here? This passage is unde-
niably foreign to twenty-first-century Western culture.
Some of us may find these words offensive because they
constitute biblical law with respect to slaves, and we
thought the Bible advocates redemption from slavery.
Well, this is a different kind of slavery than that with
which we are familiar, the kind of slavery that simply
takes people haphazardly, separating them from their
husbands, wives, and children, and putting them into
shackles and chains. That's not what is being addressed
here in Exodus. The slavery that is in view here is more
of an indentured servitude.

Let's look at the background for this type of slavery. In the first place, Jews were not allowed to enslave
other Jews in the manner in which people were taken
into captivity through military conquests. However,
there were provisions for indentured servitude in
Israel. These specifications were based on the economy
of the day. If a person incurred a debt that he could

not pay, he was not thrown into prison. Instead, he more or less hired himself out to the person to whom he owed the obligation and became a servant in order to pay off his debt by his labor. If he owed a great debt, he might need a few years to discharge it. However, the laws of Israel required that in every Sabbath year, that indentured servant had to be released, whether the debt had been fully discharged or not. The same was true every seven times seven years, when the year of jubilee occurred. Such Sabbath-year releases are in view here in Exodus 21.

What is interesting in this text is not so much the principles of indentured servitude, but the information about servants with wives. This part of the text seems particularly harsh to us. Verse 3 says, "If he comes in by himself, he shall go out by himself." That is, after the servant has worked off his debt, he's free to leave. Then the verse says, "If he comes in married, then his wife shall go out with him." That makes sense to us. But as we move into verse 4, we read, "If his master has given him a wife, and she has borne him sons or daughters, the wife and her children shall be her master's, and he shall go out by himself." That sounds like cruel and unjust treatment. The idea is that a single man owes someone a debt he can't pay, so he becomes an indentured servant to the person he owes. When the man pays his debt in full by his labor, he can leave his servitude. But if the master has given him a wife and they have had children, the wife and children can't go free with him. They can't go because, in Hebrew terms, the husband and father hasn't paid for them.

In ancient Israel, a man had to pay a dowry, or a bride price, to the father of a young woman in order to get the hand of that daughter in marriage. Of course, a man who was in debt would have no means to pay the bride price. Also, a servant working to pay off his debt would incur still more debt if his master graciously and freely gave him his daughter or one of his female servants as a wife. Therefore, when the man eventually got to the point of leaving his servitude, if he was going to be able to stay with his wife and children, he had two options. First, he could go out by himself and earn a livelihood, then come back to the master and pay the bride price, and at that time he would receive his wife and his children. Second, if he had no means to earn a living after coming out of his servitude, but he still wanted to stay with his wife and his children, he could extend his indentured servitude, not to pay the original debt that he owed, but to pay his master the bride price.

There was another, closely related custom in Israel, the custom of the so-called kinsman-redeemer. The kinsman-redeemer was a relative who could be authorized to pay off one of his relative's debts, including the bride price. We find this custom established in another somewhat unknown text in the Old Testament, Leviticus 25:23–27a:

> "The land shall not be sold permanently, for the land is Mine; for you are strangers and sojourners with Me. And in all the land of your possession you shall grant redemption of the land. If one of your brethren becomes poor, and has sold some of his possession, and if his

redeeming relative comes to redeem it, then he may redeem what his brother sold. Or if the man has no one to redeem it, but he himself becomes able to redeem it, then let him count the years since its sale, and restore the remainder to the man to whom he sold it."

What does this mean? In ancient Israel, it was the custom for a family to take care of the debts of its members. It wasn't up to the government to bail them out. If one member of the family became poor and had to sell off part of his possessions, a kinsman could come and pay the price that was owed in order to redeem that property back.

There is one Old Testament book in which the whole story is a drama centering on this practice of kinsman-redemption. It's the book of Ruth, which has special meaning to me. Inside my wedding ring is inscribed, "Your people, my people," and in my wife's wedding ring is the inscription, "Your God, my God." These words are from the book of Ruth, wherein the young Moabite woman Ruth pledges herself to go with her Israelite mother-in-law, Naomi, saying: "'Wherever you go, I will go; and wherever you lodge, I will lodge. Your people shall be my people, and your God, my God'" (Ruth 1:16b). Ruth goes to Israel with Naomi, and later in the story we meet Boaz, who acts as a kinsman-redeemer for Naomi and Ruth.

Now these terms and customs are applied throughout the Scriptures to the work of the Messiah in His atonement. In the ransom that Christ pays, He works as a Kinsman-Redeemer for His people. As our elder brother, He pays the indebtedness that we have incurred before God. He buys us out of indentured servitude by paying the price for our freedom, thereby restoring to us our inheritance in the Father's kingdom.

More important is the imagery that abounds in the New Testament with respect to the relationship between Christ and His church. The foremost image that is used for the church in the New Testament is that of the bride of Jesus Christ. This image is linked clearly to Christ's atonement, for by it He paid a ransom, a bride price, to purchase His bride. Again in this image, we see the Son of God purchasing us to secure our redemption.

The idea of a ransom, then, is woven throughout Scripture. Clearly, as we saw in the previous chapter, it was ever God's gracious intention to provide a Redeemer, One Who would pay the price to redeem us from our bondage.

Beginning in the latter part of the twentieth century, the practice of taking hostages developed as a means by which small groups of fanatics would try to influence world powers such as the United States. When this takes place, there's always a moral dilemma. If a ransom is paid to those who hold people hostage, evildoers will be encouraged to continue this despicable practice. As a result, the U.S. government established the policy of refusing to pay ransoms to hostage-takers, but rather to seek the release of hostages by other means.

God never ruled out the payment of a ransom to rescue His people from certain destruction. Christ came and paid the ransom in order to secure the release of His people, who were held captive to sin. Christ gave this ransom voluntarily, that He might redeem us from our bondage and bring us to Himself as His beloved bride.

Five

THE SAVING
SUBSTITUTE

I n the spring of 1995, I was in the stands for the decisive seventh game of the NBA's Eastern Conference championship series. The Orlando Magic were playing the Indiana Pacers. The series was knotted at three games apiece, so the winner that night would move on to the NBA finals. When we arrived, well before the opening tip-off, the noise from inside the arena was carrying all the way out to the lobby. The Orlando fans were yelling, whooping, and hollering an hour before the game was to start. As the game got under way, they just kept at it. I've never attended a sporting event where the fans made more noise than the crowd at that particular game.

As I watched the behavior of the people in the arena that night, I wondered what it is about our humanity that causes us to be so frenetic and so zealous about something like a basketball game. After all, in eternity, who will care who won or lost a sports contest? But when I looked at myself, I had to admit, "I'm here, and I care, and I'm screaming just as much as everybody else in this auditorium."

It's not unusual for us to get caught up in rooting for our favorite teams. We don't play in the games. We may not go to the games. We may not even watch them on television or listen on the radio. Even so, if we like the outcome, we have a tendency to say, "*We* won." We identify so closely with our favorite teams that when they're victorious we include ourselves in the victory. Of course, when our teams lose, we tend to change the language we use and say, "*They* lost." We let the players bear the burden and the ignominy of defeat, but we want to share in the glory of victory.

Why do we do this? In a certain sense, sports fans

experience a kind of participation. We have a sense that our teams are representing our cities, our schools, and ultimately ourselves. We may not know the players personally, but we like to think that they are doing something on our behalf, so we rejoice in their victories and agonize over their defeats. This is what is known as a *vicarious* experience.

The word *vicarious* is extremely important to our understanding of the atonement of Christ. The late Swiss theologian Karl Barth once said that, in his judgment, the single most important word in all of the Greek New Testament is the minuscule word *huper*. This little word is translated by the English phrase "in behalf of." Barth was clearly engaging in a bit of hyperbole in making this statement, because many words in the New Testament are arguably as important or even more important than *huper*, but he was simply seeking to call attention to the importance of what is known in theology as the vicarious aspect of the ministry of Jesus.

We saw earlier that Jesus' atonement has been described as a work of satisfaction. In other words,

He made satisfaction for our debt, our enmity with God, and our guilt. He satisfied the ransom demand for our release from captivity to sin. However, there is another significant word that is often used in descriptions of the atonement: *substitution*. When we looked at the biblical depiction of sin as a crime, we saw that Jesus acts as the Substitute, taking our place at the bar of God's justice. For this reason, we sometimes speak of Jesus' work on the cross as the substitutionary atonement of Christ, which means that when He offered an atonement, it was not to satisfy God's justice for His own sins, but for the sins of others. He stepped into the role of the Substitute, representing His people. He didn't lay down His life for Himself; He laid it down for His sheep. He is our ultimate Substitute.

The idea of being the Substitute in offering an atonement to satisfy the demands of God's law for others was something Christ understood as His mission from the moment He entered this world and took upon Himself a human nature. He came from heaven as the gift of the Father for the express purpose of working out redemption as our Substitute, doing for us what we could not possibly do for ourselves. We see this at the very beginning of Jesus' ministry, when He initiated His public work by coming to the Jordan River and meeting John the Baptist.

Imagine the scene at the Jordan that day. John was busy baptizing the people in preparation for the coming of the kingdom. Suddenly he looked up and saw Jesus approaching. He spoke the words that later became the lyrics for that great hymn of the church, the *Agnus Dei*: "'Behold! The Lamb of God who takes away the sin of the world!'" (John 1:29b). He announced that Jesus was the One Who had come to bear the sin of His people. In His person, He would fulfill all of what was symbolized in the Old Testament sacrificial system, by which a lamb was slaughtered and burned on the altar as an offering before God to represent atonement for sin. The lamb was a substitute, so in calling Jesus "the Lamb of God," John was asserting that He, too, would be a Substitute, but One Who would make real atonement.

Jesus came to John and, to John's horror, asked to be baptized. Scripture gives us John's reaction to this request. "John tried to prevent Him, saying, 'I need to be baptized by You, and are You coming to me?'" (Matt. 3:13). That simple statement must have masked a deep confusion on John's part. He had just announced that Jesus was the Lamb of God, and in order to serve as the perfect sacrifice to atone for the sins of His people, the Lamb of God had to be without blemish. He had to be completely sinless. But the ritual of baptism that John was calling all of Israel to undergo in preparation for the coming of the Messiah was a rite that symbolized cleansing from sin. So John said, in essence, "It would be absurd for me to baptize You, because You are the sinless Lamb of God." John then put forth an alternative idea: Jesus should baptize him. This was John's way of acknowledging that he was a sinner who needed cleansing.

Jesus overrode John's protest. "Jesus answered and said to him, 'Permit it to be so now, for thus it is fitting for us to fulfill all righteousness'" (Matt. 3:15a). Jesus' choice of words in this statement is interesting. First He said, "Permit it to be so now." The fact that Jesus gave His command to John in these particular words shows that He understood there was some theological difficulty involved. It was as if Jesus was saying, "John, I know you don't understand what's happening here, but you can trust Me. Go ahead and baptize Me."

However, Jesus went on to give an explanation as to why John should baptize Him. He said, "'It is fitting for us to fulfill all righteousness.'" The word *fitting* here can also be translated as "necessary." In other words, Jesus said it was necessary for Him to be baptized. How was it necessary? John the Baptist had come as a prophet from God. Jesus would say later, "'Among those born of women there is not a greater prophet than John the Baptist'" (Luke 7:28a). Through this prophet, God had given His covenant people a new command: they were to be baptized. We should never think that God stopped expressing His will to His people after He spoke the Tenth Commandment. A multitude of laws was added to the basic Ten Commandments after they were given. The command that His people undergo this cleansing rite to prepare for the breakthrough of the divine kingdom was merely the latest edict from God.

Before He could go to the cross, before He could fulfill the role of the Lamb of God, before He could make Himself an oblation to satisfy the demands of God's justice, Jesus had to submit Himself to every detail of every law God had given to the nation. He had to represent His people before the bar of God's justice in every detail. Since the law now required that all of the people be baptized, Jesus, too, had to be baptized. He had to fulfill every single commandment of God if He was to be sinless. He wasn't asking John to baptize Him because He needed to be cleansed; He wanted to be baptized so that He could be obedient to His Father in every detail.

That's the point Jesus was making here to John, because Jesus' mission was to be the Substitute, the vicarious sacrifice offered to God. Jesus understood this and embraced it. From the start of His ministry, He knew He had come to act as a Substitute on behalf of His sheep. At the center of His teaching was the assertion that He was doing this not for Himself but for us—to redeem us, to ransom us, to save us.

When we talk about the vicarious aspect of the

atonement, two rather technical words come up again and again: *expiation* and *propitiation*. These words spark all kinds of arguments about which one should be used to translate a particular Greek word, and some versions of the Bible will use one of these words and some will use the other one. I'm often asked to explain the difference between propitiation and expiation. The difficulty is that even though these words are in the Bible, we don't use them as part of our day-to-day vocabulary, so we aren't sure exactly what they are communicating in Scripture. We lack reference points in relation to these words.

Let's think about what these words mean, then, beginning with the word *expiation*. The prefix *ex* means "out of" or "from," so expiation has to do with removing something or taking something away. In biblical terms, it has to do with taking away guilt through the payment of a penalty or the offering of an atonement. By contrast, *propitiation* has to do with the object of the expiation. The prefix *pro* means "for," so propitiation brings about a change in God's attitude, so that He moves from being at enmity with us to being for us. Through the process of propitiation, we are restored into fellowship and favor with Him.

In a certain sense, propitiation has to do with God's being appeased. We know how the word *appeasement* functions in military and political conflicts. We think of the so-called politics of appeasement, the philosophy that if you have a rambunctious world conqueror on the loose and rattling the sword, rather than risk the wrath of his blitzkrieg you give him the Sudetenland from Czechoslovakia or some such chunk of territory. You try to assuage his wrath by giving him something that will satisfy him so that he won't come into your country and mow you down. That's an ungodly manifestation of appeasement. But if you are angry or you are violated, and I satisfy your anger, or appease you, then I am restored to your favor and the problem is removed.

The same Greek word is translated by both the words *expiation* and *propitiation* from time to time. But there is a slight difference in the terms. Expiation is the act that results in the change of God's disposition toward us. It is what Christ did on the cross, and the result of Christ's work of expiation is propitiation—God's anger is turned away. The distinction is the same as that between the ransom that is paid and the attitude of the one who receives the ransom.

Together, expiation and propitiation constitute an act of placation. Christ did His work on the cross to placate the wrath of God. This idea of placating the wrath of God has done little to placate the wrath of modern theologians. In fact, they become very wrathful about the whole idea of placating God's wrath. They think it is beneath the dignity of God to *have* to be placated, that we should have to do something to soothe Him or appease Him. We need to be very careful in how we understand the wrath of God, but let me remind you that the concept of placating the wrath of God has to do here not with a peripheral, tangential point of theology, but with the essence of salvation.

Let me ask a very basic question: what does the term *salvation* mean? We've looked at words such as *atonement, redemption, substitution, expiation,* and *propitiation.* But what does *salvation* mean in the Bible?

Trying to explain it quickly can give you a headache, because the word *salvation* is used in about seventy different ways in the Bible. If somebody is rescued from certain defeat in battle, he experiences salvation. If somebody survives a life-threatening illness, that person experiences salvation. If somebody's plants are brought back from withering to robust health, they are saved. That's biblical language, and it's really no different than our own language. We save money. A boxer is saved by the bell, meaning he's saved from losing the fight by knockout, not that he is transported into the eternal kingdom of God. In short, any experience of deliverance from a clear and present danger can be spoken of as a form of salvation.

When we talk about salvation biblically, we have to be careful to state that from which we ultimately are saved. The apostle Paul does just that for us in 1 Thessalonians 1:10, where he says Jesus "delivers us from the wrath to come." Ultimately, Jesus died to save us from the wrath of God. We simply cannot understand the teaching and the preaching of Jesus of Nazareth apart from this, for He constantly warned people that the whole world someday would come under divine judgment. Here are a few of His warnings concerning the judgment: "'I say to you that whoever is angry with his brother without a cause shall be in danger of the judgment'" (Matt. 5:22); "'I say to you that for every idle word men may speak, they will give account of it in the day of judgment'" (Matt. 12:36); and "'The men of Nineveh will rise up in the judgment with this generation and condemn it, because they repented at the preaching of Jonah; and indeed a greater than Jonah is here'" (Matt. 12:41). Jesus' theology was a crisis theology. The Greek word *crisis* means "judgment." And the crisis of which Jesus preached was the crisis of an impending judgment of the world, at which point God is going to pour out His wrath against the unredeemed, the ungodly, and the impenitent. The only hope of escape from that outpouring of wrath is to be covered by the atonement of Christ.

Therefore, Christ's supreme achievement on the cross is that He placated the wrath of God, which would burn against us were we not covered by the sacrifice of Christ. So if somebody argues against placation or the idea of Christ satisfying the wrath of God, be alert, because the gospel is at stake. This is about the essence of salvation—that as people who are covered by the atonement, we are redeemed from the supreme danger to which any person is exposed. It is a dreadful thing to fall into the hands of a holy God Who's wrathful. But there is no wrath for those whose sins have been paid. That is what salvation is all about.

In seminary, one of my classmates delivered a sermon in the chapel as part of our homiletics class. The congregation was the members of this class. At the end of the sermon, it was the role of the professor to give a summation, in front of the whole class, of all of the strengths and weaknesses of the presentation, including the content. My classmate gave a stirring sermon on the cross. This professor, however, despised orthodox Christianity and had a venomous hatred toward conservative theology, so he was belligerent and hostile after the sermon was preached. With the student standing in the pulpit after finishing his sermon, the professor challenged him, saying, "How dare you preach the substitutionary atonement in this day and age!" I couldn't believe what I was hearing. I wanted to rejoin, "What is it about this day or this age that has suddenly made the substitutionary atonement of Christ obsolete?"

I didn't do that, and I'm embarrassed that I didn't. Maybe now I understand a little better that the work that Jesus did on the cross is the very essence of the gospel. A Substitute has appeared in space and time, appointed by God Himself, to bear the weight and the burden of our transgressions, to make expiation for our guilt, and to propitiate the wrath of God on our behalf. This is the gospel. Therefore, if you take away the substitutionary atonement, you empty the cross of its meaning and drain all the significance out of the passion of our Lord Himself. If you do that, you take away Christianity itself.

Six

—

MADE LIKE HIS BRETHREN

If you were to ask a child in a typical evangelical church today to tell you what Jesus did for him, what do you suppose he would say? I can nearly guarantee that he would answer, "Jesus died for my sins." In fact, I wouldn't be surprised if you were to get that answer from the majority of adults. It's a good and true answer, of course. However, it's not a complete answer.

We have seen that the facts of God's justice and man's sinfulness combine to make an atonement absolutely necessary. We also have seen that Christ Jesus, the Son of God, the second person of the Trinity, is the One Who made satisfaction for our debt, our enmity with God, and our criminal violation of the divine law. We learned that the cross was a glorious outworking of the grace of God, by which the Father commissioned the Son to make satisfaction so that sinners might be saved with no sacrifice of God's justice. And we discovered that the Bible presents Jesus as the Redeemer, the One Who frees us from our captivity by paying a ransom for us.

However, why did it have to be Jesus? And if His work on our behalf consisted only of dying on the cross, why did He not come from heaven at age 30 and go straight to the cross? These were the questions Anselm was asking in the title of his little book *Cur Deus Homo?* (*Why the God-man?*) He was wondering why it was that God the Son had to take on humanity, be born, and live in this world for thirty-three years before making His atonement for God's people on the cross. To answer this question, we have to look further at the necessity for the atonement and then consider the requirements for the atonement.

First of all, let's go back to basics and remember that

the need for an atonement is related to the problem of human sin and the character of God—His justice and righteousness. In other words, man is unjust and God is just. In this scenario, how can these two parties ever relate?

Imagine a circle that represents the character of mankind. Now imagine that if someone sins, a spot—a moral blemish of sorts—appears in the circle, marring the character of man. If other sins occur, more blemishes appear in the circle. Well, if sins continue to multiply, eventually the entire circle will be filled with spots and blemishes. But have things reached that point? Human character is clearly tainted by sin, but the debate is about the extent of that taint. The Roman Catholic Church holds the position that man's character is not completely tainted, but that he retains a little island of righteousness. However, the Protestant Reformers of the sixteenth century affirmed that the sinful pollution and corruption of fallen man is complete, rendering us totally corrupt.

There's a lot of misunderstanding about just what the Reformers meant by that affirmation. The term that is often used for the human predicament in classical Reformed theology is *total depravity*. People have a tendency to wince whenever we use that term because there's very widespread confusion between the concept of *total* depravity and the concept of *utter* depravity. Utter depravity would mean that man is as bad, as corrupt, as he possibly could be. I don't think that there's a human being in this world who is utterly corrupt, but that's only by the grace of God and by the restraining power of His common grace. As many sins as we have committed individually, we could have done worse. We could have sinned more often. We could have committed sins that were more heinous. Or we could have committed a greater number of sins. Total depravity, then, does not mean that men are as bad as they conceivably could be.

When the Protestant Reformers talked about total depravity, they meant that sin—its power, its influence, its inclination—affects the whole person. Our bodies are fallen, our hearts are fallen, and our minds are fallen—there's no part of us that escapes the ravages of our sinful human nature. Sin affects our behavior, our thought life, and even our conversation. The whole person is fallen. That is the true extent of our sinfulness when judged by the standard and the norm of God's perfection and holiness.

To take it further, when the apostle Paul elaborates on this fallen human condition, he says, "'There is none righteous, no, not one; . . . There is none who does good; no, not one'" (Rom. 3:10b–12). That's a radical statement. Paul is saying that fallen man never, ever does a single good deed, but that flies in the face of our experience. When we look around us, we see numerous people who are not Christians who do things that we would applaud for their virtue. For instance, we see acts of self-sacrificial heroism among those who are not Christian, such as police officers and firefighters. Many people live quietly as law-abiding citizens, never defying the state. We hear regularly about acts of honesty and integrity, such as when a person returns a lost wallet rather than keeping it. John Calvin called this civil righteousness. But how can there be these deeds of apparent goodness when the Bible says that no one does good?

The reason for this problem is that when the Bible describes goodness or badness, it looks at it from two distinct perspectives. First, there is the measuring rod of the Law, which evaluates the external performance of human beings. For example, if God says you are not allowed to steal, and you go your whole life without stealing, from an external evaluation we could say that you have a good record. You've kept the Law externally.

But in addition to the external measuring rod, there is also the consideration of the heart, the internal motivation for our behavior. We're told that man judges by outward appearances, but God looks on the heart. From a biblical perspective, to do a good deed in the fullest sense requires not only that the deed conform outwardly to the standards of God's Law, but that it proceed from a heart that loves Him and wants to honor Him. You remember the great commandment: "'You shall love the Lord your God with all your heart, with all your soul, and with all your mind'" (Matt. 22:37). Is there anyone reading this book who has loved God with all of his or her heart for the past five minutes? No. Nobody loves God with all of his heart, not to mention his soul and mind.

One of the things I'm going to have to give account for on judgment day is the way in which I have wasted my mind in the pursuit of the knowledge of God. How many times have I been too lazy or slothful to apply myself to the fullest possible measure to know God? I have not loved God with all of my mind. If I loved God with all of my mind, there'd never be an impure thought in my head. But that's not the way my head works.

If we consider human performance from this perspective, we can see why the apostle would come to his apparently radical conclusion that there is no one who does good, that there's no goodness in the full sense of the word found among mankind. Even our finest works have a taint of sin mixed in. I have never done an act of charity, of sacrifice, or of heroism that came from a heart, a soul, and a mind that loved God completely. Externally, many virtuous acts are going on both among believers and unbelievers, but God considers both the external obedience and the motivation. Under that tight norm of judgment, we're in trouble.

Imagine a second circle, just like the one we had for man, to represent the character of God. How many blemishes would we see on this circle? Absolutely none. We are totally depraved, but God is absolutely holy. In fact, He is too holy to even look at iniquity. He is perfectly just.

Here, then, is the crux of the problem: how can an unjust person stand in the presence of God? Or, to put the question another way, how can an unjust person be made just, or justified? Can he start all over again? No. Once a person commits one sin, it is impossible for him ever to be perfect, because he's lost his perfection by his initial sin. Can he pay the penalty for his sin? No—unless he wishes to spend an eternity in hell. Can God simply overlook the sin? No. If God did that, He would sacrifice His justice.

Therefore, if man is to be made just, God's justice must be satisfied. Someone must be able to pay the infinite penalty for man's sin. It must be a member of the offending party, the human race, but it must be one who has never fallen into the inescapable imperfection of sin. Given these requirements, no man could qualify. However, God Himself could. For this reason, God the Son came into the world and took on humanity. As the author of Hebrews says, "He *had* to be made like His brethren . . ." (Heb. 2:17a, emphasis added).

Jesus was different from other men in at least one very significant way. Imagine a circle representing Jesus' character. He lived as a man on the earth for decades, subject to the Law of God and subject to all of the temptations known to man (Heb. 4:15). But we do not see any blemishes in His circle. Not one. This is why, as we saw in the previous chapter, John the Baptist cried, "'Behold! The Lamb of God who takes away the sin of the world!'" (John 1:29b). The Passover lambs of the Old Testament were to be lambs without blemish, as physically perfect as possible. But the ultimate lamb, the Lamb of God Who would take away the sins of His people, was to be perfect in every way. In calling Jesus the Lamb of God, John was affirming that Jesus was untouched by sin.

Jesus Himself made this claim. He asked the Pharisees, "'Which of you convicts Me of sin?'" (John 8:46a). We can become anesthetized, in a sense, by our familiarity with the New Testament stories. As a result, it sometimes happens that when Jesus says something radical, we don't even blink. How would you react if somebody said to you: "I am perfect. If you don't agree with me, prove that I'm not." That's what Jesus said. He claimed to have no shadow of turning, no blemish, no sin. He said that His meat and His drink were to do the will of the Father. He was a man Whose passion in life was obedience to the Law of God.

We have one unjust party (man) and two just parties. We have a just God, and a just Mediator, Who is altogether holy. The Mediator is the One Who came to satisfy the requirements of the just God on behalf of the unjust race of man. He is the One Who makes the unjust party just. He is the only One Who could do so.

As Protestants, the term we use for this process of making something that is unjust to be something that is just is *forensic justification*. The term *forensics* is used in the context of police investigative work or to describe high school debate matches. It has to do with authoritative formal acts of declaration. So forensic justification occurs when a person is declared to be just at the tribunal of God. This justification takes place ultimately when the supreme Judge of heaven and earth says, "You are just."

The grounds for such a declaration are in the concept of imputation. This concept is found frequently in the Scriptures, and it is central to what Jesus did on the cross. For instance, we are talking about imputation when we say that Jesus bore our sins, that He took the sins of the world on Himself. The language there is one of a quantitative act of transfer whereby the weight of guilt is taken from man and given to Christ. In other words, Christ willingly took on Himself all the blemishes on the hypothetical circle we talked about earlier in the chapter. In theological language, we say that God imputed those sins to Jesus. Therefore, God looked at Christ and saw a mass of sinfulness because all of the sins of all God's people had been transferred to the

Son. Jesus then died on the cross to make satisfaction for those sins—carrying out His roles as the Surety, the Mediator, the Substitute, and the Redeemer. That is the concept people have in mind when they say that Jesus died for them.

If all that happened was the single transfer of our sins to Jesus, we would not be justified. If Jesus took all the sins I've ever committed on His back and took the punishment for me, that would not get me into the kingdom of God. It would be good enough to keep me out of hell, but I still would not be just. I would be innocent, if you will, but still not just in a positive sense. I would have no righteousness of which to speak. We have to remember that being just is not simply being innocent, it is being righteous. It is righteousness that gets me into the kingdom of God. Jesus said that unless our righteousness exceeds that of the scribes and Pharisees, we will never get into the kingdom.

Thankfully, however, there is not just one transfer, there are two. Not only is the sin of man imputed to Christ, but the righteousness of Christ is transferred to us, to our account. As a result, in God's sight the human circle is now both clean of all blemishes and adorned with glorious righteousness. Because of that, when God declares me just, He is not lying.

We must see that the righteousness of Christ that is transferred to us is the righteousness He achieved by living under the Law for thirty-three years without once sinning. Jesus had to live a life of obedience before His death could mean anything. He had to acquire, if you will, merit at the bar of justice. Without His life of sinless obedience, Jesus' atonement would have had no value at all. We need to see the crucial significance of this truth; we need to see that not only did Jesus die for us, He lived for us.

Roman Catholics call this concept a legal fiction, and they recoil from it because they believe it casts a shadow on the integrity of God by positing that God declares to be just people who are not just. In response, the Reformers conceded that this concept would be a legal fiction if imputation were fictional. In that case, the Protestant view of justification would be a lie. But the point of the Gospel is that imputation is real—God really laid our sins on Christ and really transferred the righteousness of Christ to us. We really possess the righteousness of Jesus Christ by imputation. He is our Savior, not merely because He died, but because He lived a sinless life before He died, as only the Son of God could do.

Theologians like to employ Latin phrases, and one of my favorites is one that Martin Luther used to capture this concept. The essence of our salvation is found in this phrase: *Simul justus et pecator.* The word *simul* is the word from which we get the English word *simultaneous*; it means simply "at the same time." *Justus* is the word for "just." We all know what *et* means; we hear it in the famous words of Julius Caesar in the Shakespeare tragedy: "*Et tu, Brute?*" ("You, too, Brutus?") *Et* means "also" or "and." From the word *pecator* we get such English words as *peccadillo* ("a little sin") and *impeccable* ("without sin"); it is simply the Latin word for "sinner." So Luther's phrase, *Simul justus et pecator*, means "At the same time just and sinner."

This is the glory of the Protestant doctrine of justification. The person who is in Christ is at the very same instant a sinner and just. If I could be justified only by actually becoming just and having no sin in me, I would never see the kingdom of God. The point of the gospel is that the minute a person embraces Jesus Christ, all that Christ has done is applied to that person. All that He is becomes ours, including His righteousness. Luther was saying that at the very instant I believe, I am just by virtue of the imputation of Christ's righteousness. It's Christ's righteousness that makes me just. His death has taken care of my punishment and His life has taken care of my reward. So my justice is completely tied up in Christ.

In Protestantism, we speak of this as the doctrine of justification by faith alone, for according to the New Testament, the only means by which the righteousness and the merit of Christ can come into our accounts and be applied to us is by faith. We can't earn it. We can't deserve it. We can't merit it. We can only trust in it and cling to it.

Ultimately, however, justification by faith alone means justification by Christ alone. It's by His meritorious life and His substitutionary death that we can stand in the presence of a holy God. Without Christ, we're without hope, because all we can ever carry before God is our unjustness. But He was "born of a woman, born under the law, to redeem those who were under the law" (Gal. 4:4b–5a).

No wonder the author of Hebrews said, "How shall we escape if we neglect so great a salvation?" (Heb. 2:3a). That is a rhetorical question. The answer to the question is obvious—we will not escape at all, because it's impossible for an unjust person to survive in the presence of a just God. We need to be justified. Since we have no righteousness within us by which to be justified, we need what the Reformers called an alien or foreign righteousness. And the only such righteousness that is available is the righteousness of the God-man, Jesus Christ.

Seven

THE SUFFERING
SERVANT

The bare historical data about the crucifixion is that Jesus was executed by the Romans by being affixed to a cross outside Jerusalem. Our concern, however, is not so much with what happened but with the meaning of the crucifixion. We have noted that the atonement of Christ is a multifaceted event; that is, it can be understood in a multitude of ways: as surety for a debt, as a reconciliation of estranged parties, as judgment of a crime, or as payment of a ransom. However, it also can be "understood" in ways that have nothing to do with its true meaning.

When we turn to the Gospel records of the crucifixion events, we find participants in the story making interpretations of what they were witnessing. Those who were involved in the crucifixion of Christ and those who watched it happen understood it in widely varying ways. Without exception, those understandings were faulty.

Caiaphas, the Jewish high priest who acquiesced to the idea of Jesus' execution, understood Jesus' death as an act of political expediency. He reasoned that if the Jewish leaders allowed Jesus to be executed, they could mollify the Romans and maintain a peaceful political relationship during the imperial occupation of Judea.

The Roman governor, Pontius Pilate, gave his assessment as to what was occurring after he had interrogated Christ. He announced to the clamoring multitudes who were screaming for Jesus' blood, "'I find no fault in this Man'" (Luke 23:4b). Pilate's observation was that Jesus' condemnation was unjust from a legal standpoint, but he chose to wash his hands of the matter because he saw the crucifixion as worthwhile if it would keep the crowds pacified.

There were numerous people standing at the foot of the cross as Christ suffered. For Mary, the mother of Jesus, the crucifixion was a terrifying torment, fulfilling the prophecy she had received when she took Jesus as an infant to be dedicated in the temple (Luke 2:35). As she watched her Son die, it was as if a sword was piercing her soul. Jesus' disciples, seeing the execution of their leader, fell into despair. The crowds of ordinary people were furious because Jesus had let them down. They had expected Him to lead a revolutionary deliverance of the nation, but He had surrendered meekly to the Roman authorities. These people saw Jesus' death as a just punishment for a false pretender to the office of Messiah.

There were others with a somewhat better understanding of the crucifixion that day. A Roman centurion observed the Lord's agony and the manner of His death, and was moved to say, "'Truly this Man was the Son of God!'" (Mark 15:39b). I wish we had the opportunity to talk with him, to better understand what convinced him of Jesus' identity in this circumstance. Also, two criminals were crucified beside Jesus. One joined in the mockery of Christ, but the other responded that Jesus was an innocent man and asked Him for entrance into the kingdom.

What is missing in each of these eyewitness observations is an understanding of the crucifixion as an event of cosmic significance. That's hardly surprising. Who could have come to the conclusion, based solely on what could be seen that day on Golgotha, that Jesus was atoning for the sin of God's people? A true understanding of the crucifixion could not be reached simply by watching the event itself. Neither can we grasp the fulfillment of the cross simply by reading a record of the facts of the event. There is a need for someone to unfold the meaning behind the facts so that we will not miss the significance of the cross.

It was for this reason that Jesus sent the Holy Spirit to teach His apostles the truth about His work, that they might preach it in their own day and record it in inspired books for future generations. The New Testament epistles give us an elaborate and expansive interpretation of the meaning and significance of the historical events that are recorded for us in the gospels and in the book of Acts. It is important to note that even the gospels and Acts themselves give us more than a mere newspaper account of what took place. In them we find a certain amount of editorializing, whereby the authors give some explanation for the meaning or the significance of the events they're recording.

However, we need to realize that God did not merely provide after-the-fact interpretations of the crucifixion. For hundreds of years before Jesus was born, He gave His people prophecies about the Messiah Who would come and about the work He would accomplish. The cross was not an isolated event in history that sprang up spontaneously in a particular moment in time. It was the culmination of centuries of redemptive history. God had set certain things in motion ages and ages before, and those processes reached their zenith with the death of Christ. The Old Testament Scriptures pointed toward that zenith.

Given that scriptural record, many of those who watched as Jesus was lifted up on the cross *should* have been able to understand the significance of what they were seeing. Yet even the apostles weren't able to make these connections at the time of the crucifixion. It was only later, after the Spirit had come, that they were able to connect the dots. Thereafter, in their sermons recorded in Acts and in their letters, the apostles frequently quoted the Old Testament for help in interpreting what had occurred at Golgotha.

As we saw in an earlier chapter, the apostles had a strong precedent for using Old Testament prophesies to explain Jesus' work. Jesus Himself did just that when He went to Nazareth at the outset of His ministry and gave His inaugural sermon in the synagogue there. After reading a portion of the messianic prophecy found in Isaiah 61, Jesus said, "'Today this Scripture is fulfilled in your hearing'" (Luke 4:21). But even more striking is the manner in which Jesus taught two of His disciples about Himself on the road to Emmaus following His resurrection: "Beginning at Moses and all the Prophets, He expounded to them in *all the Scriptures* the things concerning Himself" (Luke 24:27, emphasis added). Jesus used not just Isaiah's prophecies but all of the Old Testament Scriptures to explain Himself and His ministry.

One profound example of such a use of the Scriptures by the disciples is found in the book of Acts, where Philip the deacon is able to proclaim the gospel to an Ethiopian eunuch with the help of one of the most important Old Testament prophesies of Christ. The story is found in Acts 8, beginning at verse 26:

> Now an angel of the Lord spoke to Philip, saying, "Arise and go toward the south along the road which goes down from Jerusalem to Gaza." This is desert. So he arose and went. And behold a man of Ethiopia, a eunuch of great authority under Candace the queen of the Ethiopians, who had charge of all of her treasury, and had come to Jerusalem to worship, was returning. And sitting in his chariot, he was reading Isaiah the prophet. And the Spirit said to Philip, "Go near and overtake this chariot." So Philip ran to him, and heard

him reading the prophet Isaiah, and said, "Do you understand what you are reading?"

A dignitary, the royal treasurer of the queen of Ethiopia, has been to Jerusalem to worship and is now heading home in his chariot. This isn't Ben Hur racing around the Colosseum floor, driving his horses at top speed. Rather, this man is seated comfortably as a driver attends to the procession and takes care of the horses. The Holy Spirit leads Philip to a rendezvous with the chariot and tells Philip to chase after it and to speak to this man. Providentially, he hears the Ethiopian reading aloud from the book of Isaiah. There it is—a perfect conversation-starter. So Philip asks the man whether he understands what he is reading.

And he said, "How can I, unless someone guides me?" And he asked Philip to come up and sit with him. The place in the Scripture which he read was this:

"He was led as a sheep to the slaughter;
And as a lamb before its shearer is silent,
So He opened not His mouth.
In His humiliation His justice was taken away,
And who will declare His generation?
For His life is taken from the earth."

So the eunuch answered Philip and said, "I ask you, of whom does the prophet say this, of himself or of some other man?" Then Philip opened his mouth, and beginning at this Scripture, preached Jesus to him. Now as they went down the road, they came to some water. And the eunuch said, "See here is water. What hinders me from being baptized?" Then Philip said, "If you believe with all your heart, you may." And he answered and said, "I believe that Jesus Christ is the Son of God."

This narrative in the book of Acts clearly shows the central place that Old Testament prophecy occupies in the New Testament's understanding of the death of Christ. Just as Philip did here, the apostles explained the life and work of Jesus, not from some prevailing philosophical theory, but from the Old Testament. The eunuch asks of whom Isaiah is speaking, whether it is the prophet himself or someone else, and Philip replies that he is speaking of Jesus. That's an astonishing affirmation—that hundreds and hundreds of years before Jesus was born, a prophecy was made not only about His work but about His death. No less astonishing is the effectiveness of this affirmation. In a short period of time, the Ethiopian eunuch goes from casually reading a prophecy that he can't understand without some interpretation and guidance to making a confession of faith in Christ and asking for baptism. His conversion is provoked by an application of an Old Testament text to the person and work of Christ.

Let's look more closely at the text the Ethiopian was reading. It is found in Isaiah 53, which begins with these words:

Who has believed our report?
And to whom has the arm of the Lᴏʀᴅ been
    revealed?
For He shall grow up before Him as a tender plant,
And as a root out of dry ground.

I like the imagery here. It is borrowed from the desert, where water is sparse and the arid soil mitigates against any form of vegetation. The parched earth is cracked from the heat and the aridity, and if a little shoot comes out of a crack in the floor of the desert, it struggles to survive in the noonday heat. It has very little to sustain it in the way of nutrients. This is the imagery that the prophet uses to describe the One Who will be the servant of the Lord, sometimes called the Suffering Servant, Whom God will cause to grow up out of this dry and thirsty land.

Isaiah continues with even more vivid imagery:

He has no form or comeliness;
And when we see Him,

There is no beauty that we should desire Him.
He is despised and rejected by men,
A Man of sorrows and acquainted with grief.
And we hid, as it were, our faces from Him;
He was despised, and we did not esteem Him.

When reading this passage, we wonder what Jesus really looked like in His earthly incarnation. We don't have a physical portrait of Jesus; none has survived from antiquity. There are beautiful renditions that adorn our churches, paintings that depict Christ with flowing hair, impeccable features, and so on, but those images don't seem to agree with the image that is painted for us in words here in Isaiah. The prophetic portrait of Jesus, the Messiah, the Suffering Servant, is of One Who has no form or comeliness, no beauty that He should be admired. In fact, there is something revulsive about His countenance, because according to this description, people who see Him hide their eyes from Him.

This may not refer to the normal countenance of the Suffering Servant; rather, it may refer to His ugliness during His travail leading to His execution, where

He was marred, beaten, attacked, and disfigured. But in any case, the Messiah is described as One Who is despised and rejected by men, a Man of sorrows Who is familiar with grief.

However, verses 4–6 give a critical interpretation of the mission of this One Who is so despised:

> Surely He has borne our griefs
> And carried our sorrows;
> Yet we esteemed Him stricken,
> Smitten by God, and afflicted.
> But He was wounded for our transgressions,
> He was bruised for our iniquities;
> The chastisement for our peace was upon Him,
> And by His stripes we are healed.
> All we like sheep have gone astray;
> We have turned, every one, to his own way;
> And the LORD has laid on Him the iniquity
> of us all.

This text reads almost like an eyewitness report of the crucifixion, but one of the most interesting statements here is an interpretation of the work of the Suffering Servant: "We esteemed Him stricken, smitten by God, and afflicted." What does the word *esteemed* mean in this case? As we saw when we talked about sin in an earlier chapter, we look on outward appearances, but God looks on the heart. As a result of our focus on appearances, our estimation of the meaning or significance of something can be completely wrong. But this estimation of what happened to the Suffering Servant was completely right. On the cross, God's wrath was poured out on Christ. God did strike Him, smite Him, and afflict Him—but not for any evil in Christ. He was smitten in His role as the vicarious Substitute for the people of God. This is why Isaiah declares, "He was wounded for *our* transgressions, He was bruised for *our* iniquities; the chastisement for *our* peace was upon Him, and by His stripes *we* are healed. All we like sheep have gone astray; we have turned, every one, to his own way; and the LORD has laid on Him the iniquity of *us all*" (emphasis added). The prophet labors the point of substitution.

If anything, the divine revelation through Isaiah

becomes even clearer as it moves along. Isaiah 53:10–12 reads:

> Yet it pleased the LORD to bruise Him;
> He has put Him to grief.
> When You make His soul an offering for sin,
> He shall see His seed, He shall prolong His
>   days,
> And the pleasure of the LORD shall prosper in
>   His hand.
> He shall see the labor of His soul, and be
>   satisfied.
> By His knowledge My righteous Servant shall
>   justify many,
> For He shall bear their iniquities. . . .
> And He bore the sin of many,
> And made intercession for the transgressors.

This passage contains one of my favorite verses: "He shall see the labor of His soul, and be satisfied." Here Isaiah, with extraordinary clarity, states that God the Father would look on the travail of His Son, and seeing His work on the cross, He would be satisfied. By His work as the Surety, the Mediator, the Substitute, the Redeemer, Christ would most certainly satisfy the Father's justice. His atonement would bring satisfaction.

Yet another crystal-clear prophesy of the rejection of the Messiah is found in Psalm 22, where we read:

> My God, My God, why have You forsaken
> Me?
> Why are You so far from helping Me? . . .
> But I am a worm, and no man;
> A reproach of men, and despised by the
> people.
> All those who see Me ridicule Me;
> They shoot out the lip, they shake the head,
> saying,
> "He trusted in the LORD, let Him rescue
> Him;
> Let Him deliver Him, since He delights in
> Him." . . .
> Many bulls have surrounded Me;

Strong bulls of Bashan have encircled Me.

They gape at Me with their mouths

Like a raging and roaring lion.

I am poured out like water

And all My bones are out of joint;

My heart is like wax;

It has melted within Me. . . .

For dogs have surrounded Me;

The congregation of the wicked has enclosed
Me.

They pierced My hands and My feet;

I can count all My bones.

They look and stare at Me.

They divide My garments among them,

And for My clothing they cast lots.

This psalm opens with the exact words Jesus
uttered from the cross: "My God, My God, why have
You forsaken Me?" It then goes on to mention specific
aspects of His passion: the reproach and ridicule; the
piercing of His hands and feet; the dividing of His garments; and the casting of lots by the Roman soldiers

to see which of them would get His robe. Here, then, is yet another prophesy of the Suffering Servant. Jesus obviously was familiar with this psalm and had it in mind during His atoning death. He clearly identified Himself with this particular prophetic utterance from the Old Testament.

There are many such prophesies in the Old Testament. We have already talked about Genesis 3:15, which contains the *proto-evangelium*, the first gospel, the promise that the Seed of the woman would crush the head of the serpent. Other notable messianic prophesies are found in Psalm 2, which spoke of Christ's victory; Isaiah 7:14, where Jesus' virgin birth was foretold; Isaiah 9:6–7, which made clear that the Messiah would be divine; Isaiah 11:1–10, which revealed that Jesus would come in the line of David; Isaiah 42:1–9, where the extension of the gospel to the Gentiles was prophesied; Micah 5:2, which identified the city of Jesus' birth; and Zechariah 9:9, which pictured Christ's triumphal entry. In each of these portions of Scripture, God provided clues about His intention to send One Who would take the place of His people in order to make satisfaction to God.

The Old Testament Scriptures clearly point to the atonement. They show that it was always God's intention that His Son should come into the earth in human form, live as a man under the Law, and die a substitutionary death for His people. The Gospels, in turn, give a faithful record of the events of the crucifixion, and the epistles of the New Testament then provide an inspired interpretation of the work of the Substitute, repeatedly looking back to the Old Testament. And so, by God's grace, we have at our fingertips the facts and the interpretation of those facts by which we may reach, with the Holy Spirit's enlightening aid, a true understanding of what the cross was all about.

Eight

THE BLESSING
AND THE CURSE

W hen a man is ordained to the ministry of
the gospel, one of the privileges he enjoys
is the selection of the ordination hymn. When I was
ordained to the ministry in 1965, my selection for that
occasion was "'Tis Midnight and on Olive's Brow."
The text of this hymn follows the passion of Christ
in the Garden of Gethsemane. I find that many Christians are completely unfamiliar with this particular
hymn, but I love the words—with one slight exception. At one point, the hymn declares: "Yet he that
hath in anguish knelt is not forsaken by his God."

That statement gives me pause. I can stretch my theology a little bit and say that Jesus was not forsaken by His Father in an ultimate sense, but there was a time when Jesus indeed was forsaken, and that forsakenness occurred on the cross.

Of course, Jesus Himself declared that He was forsaken in the midst of His atoning work. As we saw in the previous chapter, Jesus cried out words from Psalm 22 as He hung on the cross: "My God, My God, why have You forsaken Me?" Some have interpreted those words to indicate that Christ felt forsaken since He was in the midst of the dark night of the soul He experienced while making His atonement at Calvary, but that He was not truly abandoned by His Father. However, if Christ was not truly forsaken by His Father during His execution, then no atonement occurred, because forsakenness was the penalty for sin that God established in the old covenant. Therefore, Christ had to receive the full measure of that penalty on the cross.

To better understand this aspect of the atonement, we need to examine the cross and the work of Christ within the broader framework of what we call the covenant. I think it's impossible to have a full understanding of the death of Christ apart from an understanding of the whole process of the covenant that is worked out in the Old and New Testaments.

Those who have studied the elements of covenants in the ancient world note that although the contents of individual covenants differed from culture to culture, there were certain aspects that were virtually universal. For instance, when a legal agreement was forged, the sovereign one in the covenant would identify himself and give a historical prologue in which he rehearsed the history of his relationship to the subordinates in the covenant. This was as true for the Jews as it was for the Sumerians, the Accadians, and other peoples of antiquity.

This is why, when God made a covenant with His people, the Israelites, He first identified Himself, saying, "'I am the LORD your God, who brought you out of the land of Egypt, out of the house of bondage'" (Ex. 20:2). He gave this historical prologue, then set forth the terms of the covenant, which we call the stipulations. All covenants have stipulations. When you get married, you enter into a covenant and promise to do certain things—to love, honor, obey, and so on. When you sign an employment contract with a company, you may promise to work eight hours a day and the company promises to give you so much money, so many benefits, so much vacation time, and so forth. Those are the stipulations.

But in the ancient world, covenants also had sanctions. These would be the rewards and the penalties—rewards for keeping the stipulations of the agreement and penalties for violating the stipulations. God's covenant with Israel was no exception; it spelled out sanctions for obedience and disobedience. However, it did not use the words *rewards* and *penalties*. Under the old covenant, the reward for obedience was called a blessing and the penalty for violating the contract was called a curse.

One of the places in the Old Testament where the blessings and curses of the covenant are spelled out is Deuteronomy 28. Speaking to His people, God declares through Moses:

"Now it shall come to pass, if you diligently obey the voice of the LORD your God, to observe carefully all His commandments which I command you today, that the LORD your God will set you high above all nations of the earth. And all these blessings shall come upon you and overtake you, because you obey the voice of the LORD your God: Blessed shall you be in the city, and blessed shall you be in the country. Blessed shall be the fruit of your body, the produce of your ground and the increase of your herds, the increase of your cattle and the offspring of your flocks. Blessed shall be your basket and your kneading bowl. Blessed shall you be when you come in and blessed shall you be when you go out." (Deut. 28:1–6)

Do you see the litany? It's as if God is saying: "If you keep these terms, if you obey the commandments I have given you, I'll bless you when you stand up, I'll bless you when you sit down, I'll bless you when you roll over, I'll bless you when you're silent, I'll bless you when you speak, I'll bless you when you're in the city, I'll bless you when you're in the country, I'll bless you when you're on the highway, I'll bless you when you're on the seas. Everywhere you go, everything you do, you'll be blessed."

Then we come to the scary part, the part where it says "But . . ." Beginning in Deuteronomy 28:15 we read:

> "But it shall come to pass, if you do not obey the voice of the LORD your God, to observe carefully all His commandments and His statutes which I command you today, that all of these curses will come upon you and overtake you: Cursed shall you be in the city, and cursed shall you be in the country. Cursed shall be your basket and your kneading bowl. Cursed shall be the fruit of your body and the produce of your land, the increase of your cattle and the offspring of your flocks. Cursed shall you be when you come in, and cursed shall you be when you go out." (Deut. 28:15–19)

There are parallels here. God is saying, in effect: "If you obey, you'll be blessed. But if you disobey, you'll be cursed when you stand up, you'll be cursed when you sit down, you'll be cursed when you're in the city, you'll be cursed when you're in the country, your children will be cursed, your cattle will be cursed, your sheep will be cursed, everything will be cursed."

In order to understand these sanctions fully, we have to understand what it means to be blessed and cursed. These are important words. During the production of the New King James Version of the Bible, I attended a meeting that was called to evaluate various issues involved in the translation. One of those issues had to do with the best way to render the Beatitudes of Jesus into contemporary English. The debate was whether we should say, "Blessed are the poor in spirit . . ." or "Happy are the poor in spirit. . . ." There were a number of people at that meeting who wanted the translation to say "happy," but I protested because there is a special theological significance to the word *blessed* that is not connoted in the English word *happy*. My concern was that if we were to translate

125

that particular Bible with the English word *happy*, we would leave the content poverty-stricken. Thankfully, the majority of those in attendance that day agreed that the word *blessed* should be used, so today the New King James Version says that the poor in spirit are "blessed."

What, then, is the significance of this word? To the Jew, blessedness meant receiving supreme favor from the hands of God. My favorite way of explaining supreme favor is to look at the Hebrew benediction, found in Numbers 6:24–26. God commanded the priests of Israel to bless the people with these words:

"The Lord bless you and keep you;
The Lord make His face shine upon you,
And be gracious to you;
The Lord lift up His countenance upon
   you,
And give you peace."

Notice that in this benediction there is a poetic structure. It is a form of literature called synthetic parallelism. There are three verses, and each of them essentially means the same thing. Different words are employed for poetic richness and diversity, but the message is the same. Moreover, this parallelism helps us understand the Jewish view of blessedness. Notice that the first part of the first statement reads, "The LORD bless you." Thanks to the parallelism, we can then get a clue to what divine blessing was by looking at the first parts of each of the next two statements. We find that blessedness was equivalent to the face of God shining upon you and God lifting up the light of His countenance upon you.

For the Jew, then, the supreme blessedness was the Beatific Vision, the *Visio Dei*, the vision of God, looking God in the face. If we were to study that carefully in all its ramifications in the Old Testament, we would see that blessedness is related to proximity of God's presence. The closer one gets to the immediate presence of God, the greater the blessedness. The farther removed a person is from the face of God, the less the blessedness.

A curse is the opposite of a blessing. So the supreme

form of cursedness is for the Lord to turn His back on you and bring judgment on you.

The concept of blessedness in the Old Testament was understood in terms of the nearness, the proximity, to the presence of God. Conversely, the curse of the covenant was to be cut off from the presence of God, never to see the light of His countenance, to be cast into the outer darkness. That's how the Jew understood the curse.

This idea is in the background of many Old Testament events and rituals. For instance, during the time of Israel's wilderness wanderings after the deliverance from Egypt, the people encamped in a special way. They pitched their tents according to a pattern that God gave them for the arrangement of the tribes. The tents were all arranged around a central point. At the center stood the tabernacle. God pitched His tent in the middle, right in the midst of the people. His presence was with the Israelites. It's not surprising that the Jews developed an image of Gentiles as "outsiders," for they lived outside the camp of the covenant people, in the "outer darkness."

Another illustration of this understanding is seen in the Old Testament ceremony of the Day of Atonement. On that day each year, a lamb was sacrificed on the altar as a blood offering for the sins of the people, but the ceremony also involved a goat, the scapegoat. The sins of the nation were ceremonially transferred to the head of the goat, and then a significant thing happened. The goat was not killed—that symbolism was taken care of with the lamb. Rather, the goat was sent outside the camp. It was driven into the wilderness, into the place of darkness, into a place removed from the light of God's countenance. In other words, the goat was cursed.

Let's skip forward to the New Testament letter of the apostle Paul to the Galatians. Quoting Deuteronomy 27:26, Paul writes, "Cursed is everyone who does not continue in all things which are written in the book of the law, to do them" (Gal. 3:10b). By quoting this Old Testament passage, Paul shows that anyone who relies on observing the Law to achieve a relationship with God, who trusts in his own good works and his own performance, is bound to experience cursedness, for God's standard is perfection, which no fallen human being can achieve. Then Paul writes, "Christ has redeemed us from the curse of the law, having become a curse for us (for it is written, 'Cursed is everyone who hangs on a tree')" (Gal. 3:13b). Paul is saying that on the cross, Christ became a curse for us, that He bore all of the sanctions of the covenant, and he paraphrases Deuteronomy 21:22–23: "Cursed is everyone who hangs on a tree."

If we look at the intricacy of the drama of the events of Jesus' crucifixion, we see that some amazing things took place so that Old Testament prophetic utterances were fulfilled to the minutest detail. In the first instance, the Old Testament said that the Messiah would be delivered to the Gentiles ("dogs" or "congregation of the wicked") for judgment (Ps. 22:16). It just so happened in the course of history that Jesus was put on trial during a time of Roman occupation of Palestine. The Romans allowed a certain amount of home rule by their conquered vassals, but they did not permit the death penalty to be imposed by the local rulers, so the Jews did not have the authority to put Christ to death. The only thing they could do was to meet in council and take Jesus to Pontius Pilate, the Roman governor, asking him to carry out the execution. So Jesus was delivered from His own people to the Gentiles—those who were "outside the camp." He was delivered into the hands of pagans who dwelt outside the arena in which the face of God shone, outside the circle of the light of His countenance.

Second, the site of Jesus' execution was outside Jerusalem. Once He was judged by the Gentiles and condemned to be executed, He was led out of the fortress, onto the Via Dolorosa, and outside the walls of the city. Just as the scapegoat was driven outside the camp, Jesus was taken outside Zion, outside the holy city where the presence of God was concentrated. He was sent into the outer darkness.

Third, whereas the Jews did their executions by stoning, the Romans did them by crucifixion. That determined the method of Jesus' death: He would hang on a tree—a cross made of wood. The Bible doesn't say, "Cursed is everyone who is stoned." It says, "Cursed is everyone who hangs on a tree."

Fourth, when Jesus was put on the cross, there was an astronomical perturbation. In the middle of the afternoon, it became dark. Darkness descended on the land. By some method, perhaps by an eclipse, the sun was blotted out. It was as if God had veiled the light of His countenance.

In the midst of the intensity of this darkness, Jesus cried out, "My God, My God, why have You forsaken Me?" This was one of the most striking utterances that came from the lips of Jesus while He was on the cross, and there have been all kinds of interpretations of it. Albert Schweitzer looked at that cry and said it was proof positive that Jesus died in disillusionment. According to Schweitzer, Jesus had expectations that God would deliver Him, but God let Him down in the final moments, so Jesus died as a disillusioned, tragic Shakespearean hero. Others have noticed, as we mentioned in the previous chapter, that these words are found verbatim in Psalm 22, and they conclude that Jesus was identifying Himself with the Suffering Servant of Psalm 22 and was reciting poetry at His death. But that misses all the indications—Jesus' executioners, the place of His execution, the manner of His execution, the darkness that fell—that so clearly tell us that Jesus cried out to His Father because He actually had been forsaken.

The sign of the old covenant was circumcision. This cutting of the foreskin had two significances, one positive and one negative, corresponding to the two sanctions. On the positive side, the cutting of the foreskin symbolized that God was cutting out a group of people from the rest, separating them, setting them apart to be a holy nation. The negative aspect was that the Jew who underwent circumcision was saying, "Oh, God, if I fail to keep every one of the terms of this covenant, may I be cut off from You, cut off from Your presence, cut off from the light of Your countenance, cut off from Your blessedness, just as I have now ritually cut off the foreskin of my flesh."

The cross was the supreme circumcision. When Jesus took the curse on Himself and so identified with our sin that He became a curse, God cut Him off, and justly so. At the moment when Christ took on Himself the sin of the world, His figure on the cross was the most grotesque, most obscene mass of concentrated sin in the history of the world. God is too holy to look on iniquity, so when Christ hung on the cross, the Father, as it were, turned His back. He averted His face and He cut off His Son. Jesus, Who, touching His human nature, had been in a perfect, blessed relationship with God throughout His ministry, now bore the sin of God's people, and so He was forsaken by God.

Imagine how agonizing that was for Christ. Thomas Aquinas argued that throughout His earthly ministry, Jesus remained in a constant state of intimate communion with His Father. Aquinas speculated that the Beatific Vision, the vision of the unveiled glory of God, was something Jesus had enjoyed every minute of His life until the cross, when the light was turned off. The world was plunged into darkness, and Christ was exposed to the curse of the wrath of God. To experience the curse, according to Jewish categories, was to experience what it means to be forsaken.

I've heard sermons about the nails and the thorns.

Granted, the physical agony of crucifixion is a ghastly thing. But thousands of people have died on crosses, and others have had even more painful, excruciating deaths than that. But only One received the full measure of the curse of God while on a cross. Because of that, I wonder whether Jesus was even aware of the nails and the thorns. He was overwhelmed by the outer darkness. On the cross, He was in hell, totally bereft of the grace and the presence of God, utterly separated from all blessedness of the Father. He became a curse for us so that we one day will be able to see the face of God. God turned His back on His Son so that the light of His countenance will fall on us. It's no wonder Jesus screamed from the depths of His soul.

Finally, Jesus said, "'It is finished!'" (John 19:30b). What was finished? His life? The pain of the nails? No. The lights had come back on; God's countenance had turned back. So Jesus could say, "'Father, into Your hands I commit My spirit'" (Luke 23:46b).

The hard reality is this: if Jesus was not forsaken on the cross, we are still in our sins. We have no redemption, no salvation. The whole point of the cross was for Jesus to bear our sins and bear the sanctions of the covenant. In order to do that, He had to be forsaken. Jesus submitted Himself to His Father's will and endured the curse, that we, His people, might experience the ultimate blessedness.

Nine

A SECURE FAITH

When I lived and ministered in western Pennsylvania, the residents of the small town of Greensburg became upset about some work that was done by the Pennsylvania Department of Transportation. It seemed that a crew from the department painted new white lines down the center of the highway outside Greensburg, and then another crew came and put a fresh asphalt topping over the new white lines. Not surprisingly, the taxpayers were scratching their heads about this kind of procedure.

You may wonder what this story has to do with

the atonement. There has been a great controversy in the history of the church concerning the intent of God the Father and of God the Son in the act of the atonement. The question is, "For whom did Christ die?" In other words, what was God's design and purpose in the whole dynamic activity of the cross? In my opinion, some responses to that question function just like the Pennsylvania Department of Transportation—they paint white lines, then cover them up.

The Reformed branch of the church has answered this question with the doctrine of limited atonement, also known as the doctrine of particular redemption. When people hear of limited atonement, they immediately tend to think of Calvinism, because the idea of limited atonement is linked historically to the name *John Calvin* and the term *Calvinism*. Indeed, the doctrine of limited atonement is one of the so-called "five points of Calvinism."

It is somewhat of a misnomer to speak of Calvinism as having five points. Calvin himself did not summarize Reformed theology by listing five points. Nowhere in his voluminous writings will you find such a summation of his theology. The five points actually were compiled in Holland in the seventeenth century, when there was a reaction among Dutch clergymen to their own historic brand of Calvinism. A group led by James Arminius protested against certain doctrines that were part of orthodox Reformed theology. These protesters, who were called the Remonstrants, listed five particular doctrines of Reformed theology with which they disagreed. The Synod of Dort was called to answer the complaints of the Remonstrants, and the delegates to that synod reaffirmed historic Reformed theology and repudiated the Remonstrants' positions. In doing so, they summarized the classical Reformed position on each of the five points the Remonstrants had questioned, and since then we've heard of the five points of Calvinism. Reformed theology teaches a lot more than five points, but these five points are definite distinctives of Calvinistic doctrine.

It is important to note that the doctrine of limited atonement was not introduced by Calvin and is not unique to Calvinism. The debate over the atonement intensified as early as the fourth century, when the focus was on the teachings of Augustine over against those of the British monk Pelagius. It was Augustine who most clearly articulated the concept in a theological way for the early church fathers. In fact, Calvinism is really just a later synonym for Augustinianism, which we touched on briefly in Chapter 1.

In any case, these five singular points of Calvinistic doctrine are often summarized by the acronym TULIP, with each letter standing for one of the five points. The T stands for total depravity, the U is for unconditional election, the L signifies limited atonement, the I is for irresistible grace, and the P stands for the perseverance of the saints.

Each of these doctrines is questioned and debated by many in the church, but I doubt that any of these five points has created more controversy than the L. In fact, there are hosts of folks who call themselves four-point Calvinists because they just can't swallow the doctrine of limited atonement. Sometimes they say, "I'm not a Calvinist and I'm not an Arminian, I'm a Calminian." I think that a four-point Calvinist *is* an Arminian. I say that for this reason: When I have talked to people who call themselves four-point Calvinists and have had the opportunity to discuss it with them, I have discovered that they were no-point Calvinists. They thought they believed in total depravity, in unconditional election, in irresistible grace, and in the perseverance of the saints, but they didn't understand these points.

Only once have I encountered an exception to this general rule, one self-proclaimed four-point Calvinist who was *not* a no-point Calvinist. This person happened to be a teacher of theology. I was interested in his position, so I said to him: "I want to hear how you handle this, because I trust you. I know you're knowledgeable in theology, and I want to hear how you think this through." I expected that he would not have an accurate understanding of the T, U, I, and P. But to my astonishment, when he went through them, I found that he had them down as clearly as any strict Calvinist ever articulated them. I was rejoicing, but I was also amazed. I said, "Now tell me about your understanding of limited atonement." When he gave me his understanding of limited atonement, I discovered this man was not a four-point Calvinist, he was a five-point Calvinist. He believed in limited atonement and didn't know it.

My point is that there is confusion about what the doctrine of limited atonement actually teaches. However, I think that if a person really understands the other four points and is thinking at all clearly, he *must* believe in limited atonement because of what Martin Luther called a resistless logic. Still, there are people who live in a happy inconsistency. I believe it's possible for a person to believe four points without believing the fifth, although I don't think it's possible to do it consistently or logically. However, it is certainly a possibility given our proclivity for inconsistency.

To begin to unravel the misconceptions about this doctrine, let's look first at the question of the value of the atoning sacrifice of Jesus Christ. Classical Augustinianism teaches that the atonement of Jesus Christ is *sufficient* for all men. That is, the sacrifice Christ offered to the Father is of infinite value. There is enough merit in the work of Jesus to cover the sins of every human being who has ever lived and ever will live. So there is no limit to the value of the sacrifice

He made. There is no debate about this.

Calvinists make a distinction between the *sufficiency* and the *efficiency* of the atonement. That distinction leads to this question: was Jesus' death efficient for everybody? In other words, did the atonement result in everyone being saved automatically? Jesus' work on the cross was valuable enough to save all men, but did His death actually have the effect of saving the whole world?

This question has been debated for centuries, as noted above. However, if the controversy over limited atonement was only about the value of the atonement, it would be a tempest in a teapot because the distinction between the sufficiency and efficiency of the atonement does not define the difference between historic Reformed theology and non-Reformed views such as Semi-Pelagianism and Arminianism. Rather, it merely differentiates between universalism and particularism. Universalists believe that Jesus' death on the cross *did* have the effect of saving the whole world. Calvinism disagrees strongly with this view, but historic Arminianism and dispensationalism also repudiate universalism. Each of these schools of thought agrees that Christ's atonement is particular and not universal in the sense that it works or effects salvation only for those who believe in Christ, so that the atonement does not automatically save everybody. Therefore, the distinction between the sufficiency and efficiency of Jesus' work defines particularism, but not necessarily the concept of limited atonement.

As an aside, let me say that while not everyone is saved by the cross, the work of Christ yields universal or near-universal concrete benefits. Through the death of Christ, the church was born, which led to the preaching of the gospel, and wherever the Gospel is preached there is an increase in virtue and righteousness in society. There is a spillage from the influence of the church, which brings benefits to all men. Also, people around the world have benefited from the church's commitment to hospitals, orphanages, schools, and so on.

The real heart of the controversy over limited atonement is this question: what was God's intent or His design in sending Christ to the cross? Was it the purpose of the Father and the Son to make an atonement that would be made available to all who would put their trust in it, with the possibility that none might avail themselves of its benefits? In other words, was God's purpose in sending Christ to the cross simply to make salvation *possible*? Or did God from all eternity plan to send Christ to die a substitutionary death in order to effect an *actual* atonement that would be applied to certain elect individuals?

Historic Reformed theology takes the biblical doctrine of divine election seriously. Because of it, Calvinists believe that God had a plan from all eternity to redeem a people for Himself. That plan encompassed only a portion of the human race; it was never God's intention to save everybody. Remember, given our sin and His justice, God was under no obligation to save anyone. Indeed, He would have been perfectly just if He had consigned all people to eternal damnation, but in His mercy, He chose to save some. If it had been God's intention to save everybody, then everybody would be saved, but God's purpose in redemption was to save a remnant of the human race from the wrath they had earned for themselves and justly deserved.

These people will receive God's mercy; all others will receive His justice.

The design of the atonement was that Christ would go to the cross, as He Himself said, as "'a ransom for many'" (Matt. 20:28b). He would lay down His life, as He said, "'for the sheep'" (John 10:11b). The purpose of the atonement was to provide salvation for God's elect. Simply put, Reformed theology teaches that Jesus Christ went to the cross for the elect, and only for the elect. That, in a nutshell, is the doctrine of limited atonement.

People have trouble with that, particularly if I use those words to describe the doctrine. What if I say Jesus went to the cross to make an atonement for believers, and only for believers? In that statement, I declare that it was God's design that Jesus should die not for everybody indiscriminately, but only for those who would believe. If you accept that, you see that only the elect are believers and that only believers are the elect. I'm not saying anything different when I say that Christ died only for the elect. Can you conceive of people who are believers who are not elect, or of people who are elect who are not believers? That kind of disjunction is utterly foreign to the New Testament.

Many other objections are raised to limited atonement. One of the major stumbling blocks is Scripture's own statements that Jesus died for "the world." Such statements must always be weighed against other biblical propositions that clearly state specifically for whom Jesus died. Also, we must strive to gain a true understanding of the meaning of the word *world* in the Bible. The point the New Testament writers were making, particularly to a Jewish audience, is that Jesus is not just the Savior of Jewish people, but that people from every tongue, race, and nation are numbered among the elect. In other words, the atonement has implications for the whole world, but that doesn't mean each and every person in the world is saved. That can't be drawn from the text.

Some people react against the doctrine of limited atonement because it appears to take away from the greatness of the work of Christ. In reality, it's the Arminian position that diminishes and devalues the full impact and power of the atonement. The point Calvinists stress is that Christ accomplished what He set out to accomplish, the job the Father had designed for Him to do. God's sovereign will is not at the whim and mercy of our personal and individual responses to it. If it were, there is a theoretical possibility that God's plan could be thwarted and, in the end, no one might be saved. For the Arminian, salvation is possible for all but certain for none. In the Calvinist position, salvation is sure for God's elect.

Another frequently cited objection is that the doctrine of limited atonement undermines evangelism. All orthodox Christians, Calvinists included, believe and teach that the atonement of Jesus Christ is to be proclaimed to all men. We are to say that God so loved the world that He gave His only begotten Son, that whoever believes on Him should not perish but have everlasting life. The misconception exists that because Calvinists believe in the doctrine of limited atonement, they have no passion to go out and preach the cross to everyone. Calvinists have been careful since Augustine to insist that the gospel is to be offered to all men—even though we know that not everyone will respond to it. Many Calvinists have been zealous evangelists.

The doctrine of limited atonement, in reality, is helpful in evangelism. The Calvinist knows that not everyone will respond to the gospel message, but he also knows with certainty that some will respond to it. By contrast, the Arminian doesn't know that not everyone will respond. In the Arminian's mind, it's a theoretical possibility that everybody will repent and believe. However, the Arminian also must deal with the possibility that no one will respond. He can only hope that his gospel presentation will be so persuasive that the unbeliever, lost and dead in his trespasses and sins, will choose to cooperate with divine grace so as to take advantage of the benefits offered in the atonement.

If we can get past such perceived problems with the doctrine of limited atonement, we can begin to see the glory of it—that the atonement Christ made on the cross was real and effectual. It wasn't just a hypothetical atonement. It was an actual atonement. He didn't offer a hypothetical expiation for the sins of His people; their sins *were* expiated. He didn't give a hypothetical propitiation for our sins; He actually placated God's wrath toward us. By contrast, according to the other view, the atonement is only a potentiality. Jesus went to the cross, paid the penalty for sin, and made the atonement, but now He sits in heaven wringing His hands and hoping that someone will take advantage of the work He performed. This is foreign to the biblical understanding of the triumph and the victory Christ achieved in His atoning death.

In His High Priestly Prayer in John 17:6–9a, Jesus said:

> "I have manifested Your name to the men whom You have given Me out of the world. They were Yours, You gave them to Me, and they have kept Your word. Now they have known that all things which You have given Me are from You. . . . They have . . . known surely that I came forth from You; and they have believed that You sent Me. I pray for them."

This was Jesus, the Savior, speaking here. Notice that He said He was praying for His disciples—not for the world. In the most poignant prayer of intercession He offered in this world as our High Priest, Jesus explicitly said He was *not* praying for everybody. Instead, He was praying for the elect.

Is it conceivable that Jesus would be willing to die for the whole world but not pray for the whole world? That doesn't make sense. He was being consistent. He had come to lay down His life for His sheep. He was going to die for His people, and He made it clear here that those were the ones for whom He was about to die. There is no question here of indiscrimination. Jesus was about to make atonement, and that atonement would be effective for everyone for whom He intended it to be effective.

If you are of the flock of Christ, one of His lambs, then you can know with certainty that an atonement has been made for your sins. You may wonder how you can know you're numbered among the elect. I cannot read your heart or the secrets of the Lamb's Book of Life, but Jesus said: "'My sheep hear My voice'" (John 10:27a). If you want Christ's atonement to avail for you, and if you put your trust in that atonement and rely on it to reconcile you to almighty God, in a practical sense, you don't need to worry about the abstract questions of election. If you put your trust in Christ's death for your redemption and you believe on the Lord Jesus Christ, then you can be sure that the atonement was made for you. That, more than anything else, will settle for you the question of the mystery of God's election. Unless you're elect, you won't believe on Christ; you won't embrace the atonement or rest on His shed blood for your salvation. If you want it, you can have it. It is offered to you if you believe and if you trust.

One of the sweetest statements from the lips of Jesus in the New Testament is this: "'Come, you blessed of My Father, inherit the kingdom prepared for you from the foundation of the world'" (Matt. 25:34b). There is a plan of God designed for your salvation. It is not an afterthought or an attempt to correct a mistake. Rather, from all eternity, God determined that He would redeem for Himself a people, and that which He determined to do was, in fact, accomplished in the work of Jesus Christ, His atonement on the cross. Your salvation has been accomplished by a Savior Who is not merely a potential Savior but an actual Savior, One Who did for you what the Father determined He should do. He is your Surety, your Mediator, your Substitute, your Redeemer. He atoned for your sins on the cross.

Ten

QUESTIONS AND ANSWERS

In this final chapter, I would like to touch briefly on various other issues surrounding the atonement:

WHAT IS THE SIGNIFICANCE OF THE SHEDDING OF BLOOD IN THE ATONEMENT?

The idea that there's some intrinsic or inherent power in the blood of Jesus is a popular concept in the Christian world. It even crops up from time to time in various hymns and praise songs. This idea reflects a fundamental misunderstanding of the concept of the blood as it relates to atonement from a biblical perspective.

I once heard my dear friend John Guest, who is an Anglican evangelist, preach on the cross and the blood of Christ. He asked this question: "Had Jesus come to this earth and scratched His finger on a nail so that a drop or two of blood was spilled, would that have been sufficient to redeem us? That would have constituted the shedding of blood. If we're saved by the blood of Christ, wouldn't that have been enough?" Obviously the point John was trying to make is that it's not the blood of Christ as such that saves us.

The significance of blood in the sacrificial system is that it represents life. The Old Testament repeatedly makes the point that "the life of the flesh is in the blood" (Lev. 17:11). Therefore, when the blood is poured out, the life is poured out. That's significant, because under the covenant of works in the Garden of Eden, the penalty that was laid down for disobedience was death. God required that penalty for sin. That is why Jesus had to die to accomplish the atonement. When the blood is shed and the life is poured out, the penalty is paid. Nothing short of that penalty will do.

JESUS WAS FORSAKEN BY HIS FATHER ON THE CROSS. SIMILARLY, WE SOMETIMES HEAR IT SAID THAT THOSE IN HELL ARE FORSAKEN BY GOD IN THE SENSE THAT HELL IS THE ABSENCE OF GOD. SCRIPTURE CLEARLY TEACHES THAT GOD IS OMNIPRESENT. DAVID SAID, "IF I MAKE MY BED IN HELL, BEHOLD, YOU ARE THERE" (PS. 139:8B). HOW, THEN, ARE WE TO UNDERSTAND HELL AND THE PRESENCE OF GOD?

It is common to say that hell is the absence of God. Such statements are motivated in large part by the dread of even contemplating what hell is like. We try to soften that blow and find a euphemism to skirt around it.

We need to realize that those who are in hell desire nothing more than the absence of God. They didn't want to be in God's presence during their earthly lives, and they certainly don't want Him near when they're in hell. The worst thing about hell is the presence of God there.

When we use the imagery of the Old Testament in

an attempt to understand the forsakenness of the lost, we are not speaking of the idea of the departure of God or the absence of God in the sense that He ceases to be omnipresent. Rather, it's a way of describing the withdrawal of God in terms of His redemptive blessing. It is the absence of the light of His countenance. It is the presence of the frown of His countenance. It is the absence of the blessedness of His unveiled glory that is a delight to the souls of those who love Him, but it is the presence of the darkness of judgment. Hell reflects the presence of God in His mode of judgment, in His exercise of wrath, and that's what everyone would like to escape.

I think that's why we get confused. There is a withdrawal in terms of the blessing of the radical nearness of God. His benefits can be removed far from us, and that's what this language is calling attention to.

THE FAMOUS HYMN OF THE CHURCH "AND CAN IT BE?" CONTAINS A LINE THAT ASKS A VERY POIGNANT QUESTION: "HOW CAN IT BE THAT THOU, MY GOD, SHOULDST DIE FOR ME?"

IS IT ACCURATE TO SAY THAT GOD DIED ON THE CROSS?

This kind of expression is popular in hymnody and in grassroots conversation. So although I have this scruple about the hymn and it bothers me that the expression is there, I think I understand it, and there's a way to give an indulgence for it.

We believe that Jesus Christ was God incarnate. We also believe that Jesus Christ died on the cross. If we say that God died on the cross, and if by that we mean that the divine nature perished, we have stepped over the edge into serious heresy. In fact, two such heresies related to this problem arose in the early centuries of the church: *theopassianism* and *patripassianism*. The first of these, *theopassianism*, teaches that God Himself suffered death on the cross. *Patripassianism* indicates that the Father suffered vicariously through the suffering of His Son. Both of these heresies were roundly rejected by the church for the very reason that they categorically deny the very character and nature of God, including His immutability. There is no change in the substantive nature or character of God at any time.

God not only created the universe, He sustains it by the very power of His being. As Paul said, "In Him we live and move and have our being" (Acts 17:28). If the being of God ceased for one second, the universe would disappear. It would pass out of existence, because nothing can exist apart from the sustaining power of God. If God dies, everything dies with Him. Obviously, then, God could not have perished on the cross.

Some say, "It was the second person of the Trinity Who died." That would be a mutation within the very being of God, because when we look at the Trinity we say that the three are one in essence, and that though there are personal distinctions among the persons of the Godhead, those distinctions are not essential in the sense that they are differences in being. Death is something that would involve a change in one's being.

We should shrink in horror from the idea that God actually died on the cross. The atonement was made by the human nature of Christ. Somehow people tend to think that this lessens the dignity or the value of the substitutionary act, as if we were somehow implicitly denying the deity of Christ. God forbid. It's the

God-man Who dies, but death is something that is experienced only by the human nature, because the divine nature isn't capable of experiencing death.

IS THERE A CONNECTION BETWEEN A FAULTY UNDERSTANDING OF MAN'S DEPRAVITY AND REJECTION OF THE DOCTRINE OF LIMITED ATONEMENT?

At the risk of sounding like a broken record because I've said it so many times, I really think that the biggest problem we have in theology is achieving a correct understanding of two doctrines—the doctrine of God and the doctrine of man. In the *Institutes of the Christian Religion*, in the opening chapter, John Calvin writes about the importance of having a sound understanding of who man is in order to gain a proper understanding of Who God is. He then makes a somewhat paradoxical statement and says that in order to understand man, you have to understand God, too. Unfortunately, we don't know Who God is, so we don't know who we are, but the more we understand of the holiness and the righteousness of God, the more we begin to see by contrast how desperately fallen we are and how utterly dependent we are on His mercy and grace.

The basic conflict in theology is between a theocentric theology and an anthropocentric theology—a God-centered theology or a man-centered theology. I'm afraid that many professing Christians are much more concerned about the exaltation of human beings than they are about the dignity of God Himself.

DO YOU SEE ANY CONFLICT BETWEEN "DECISION SALVATION" AND ELECTION?

I think the biggest danger is that churches are filled with people who have made a profession of faith but are not in a state of grace. Justification is by the possession of faith, and anyone who possesses it is certainly called to profess it. But you don't get into the kingdom of God by raising your hand, by walking down an aisle, by praying a prayer, or by signing a card. All of these acts are good, but they're externals. Unfortunately, we tend to focus on these things. When someone makes a profession, we say, "You're in." We don't ask the person to examine himself or herself to see whether the faith he or she is professing is authentic faith. But it's vital that we do so, because only authentic faith will bring justification. Such faith is the gift of God. I can never provoke faith in another. I can plant a seed and I can water the seed that has been planted, but only God the Holy Spirit can bring forth the increase.

HOW DOES TODAY'S POSTMODERNISM AFFECT THE POPULAR UNDERSTANDING OF THE ATONEMENT?

My biggest concern is the way in which the postmodern mentality is seducing the church, even the Reformed church. There seems to be a tacit assumption that somewhere around 1970, at the end of the cultural revolution of the 1960s, that something remarkable happened—a constituent change took place in the nature of human beings, from the manner in which we were created. Now life is no longer constructed on the basis of truth piercing the soul by way of the mind. Since about 1970, we have adopted a "sensuous culture" that is all about feelings, about relationships, about everything subjective. Even truth itself is regarded as subjective rather than objective. Therefore, truth is whatever you want it to be. This is the most narcissistic generation in the history of the human race.

Driven by these changes, churches are rushing to alter their approach to the culture, adopting the use of sound bites, entertainment, and that sort of thing. They are forgetting that the power is in the Word of God, not in methods, and that the Word is addressed in the first instance to the mind. The Word was intended by God to be intelligible, and only as we understand it does it get into our bloodstreams and into our hearts, and show up in changed lives.

WE SPEAK ABOUT THE ATONEMENT OF CHRIST, BUT IT WAS GOD THE FATHER WHO SENT JESUS INTO THE WORLD. WHAT CAN WE DO TO BOLSTER OUR UNDERSTANDING OF THE CENTRALITY OF THE FATHER IN REDEMPTIVE HISTORY?

In practical terms, I think one of the best and most important things we can do is to revisit the Old Testament. One of my pet peeves is the way in which we think that since the gospel has appeared in history and the New Testament portrait of Jesus has come, we can now disregard or dispense with the Old Testament. We forget that this huge body of information is divine revelation, and much of the content of that revelation is an unveiling for our benefit of the character of God. We need to meet the God of the Old Testament, because it is He Whom Jesus called Father. It was the Old Testament God Who sent Jesus into the world and Who was satisfied by the atonement of Christ.

We call ourselves Christians rather that "Godians," but we need to remember that the reason we love Jesus and follow Him is that He has reconciled us to the Father. Jesus Himself is subordinate in the economy of redemption to the Father, and He calls us to *soli Deo gloria,* to give the glory where it belongs, to God.

AT WHAT POINT IN HISTORY IS AN INDIVIDUAL PERSON REDEEMED—WHEN CHRIST DIED ON

THE CROSS FOR HIS PEOPLE OR WHEN THE INDIVIDUAL RESPONDS TO THE GOSPEL IN FAITH?

In the Greek version of the Bible, the verb "to save" appears in every possible tense. It is said that we *were saved* from the foundation of the world, that we *were being saved* from the foundation of the world, that we *are saved*, that we *are being saved*, that we *shall be saved*, and so on. The point is that from the foundation of the world we were justified in the decrees of God, but that was not accomplished until the space and time work of Christ and it is not realized subjectively until we are quickened by the Holy Spirit to come to faith and appropriate the benefits that were determined and secured for us in ages past.

DID THE ATONEMENT APPLY TO THOSE WHO LIVED BEFORE THE CRUCIFIXION OF CHRIST?

The answer to this question is clear from Scripture. The people who lived in Old Testament times had the sacrificial system, but the blood of bulls and goats didn't atone for anyone. These things pointed the people of Israel beyond themselves to an atonement that would satisfy the righteousness of God. The Old Testament person who trusted the promise of the work of the Messiah, even though that work had not yet been accomplished in space and time, was saved. The ground of that salvation was the work of Christ that was yet to come. Old Testament believers were saved by a faith that looked forward, while we are saved by a faith that looks backward. The objective ground for the salvation of both groups is the same—the atonement of Christ.

ABOUT THE AUTHOR

Dr. R. C. Sproul is the founder and chairman of Ligonier Ministries, an international multimedia ministry based in Lake Mary, Florida. He also serves as senior minister of preaching and teaching at Saint Andrew's Chapel in Sanford, Florida.

During his distinguished academic career, Dr. Sproul has helped train men for the ministry as a professor at Reformed Theological Seminary and later at Knox Theological Seminary.

He is the author of more than sixty books, including *The Holiness of God, Chosen by God, What Is Reformed Theology?, The Invisible Hand, Faith Alone*, and *A Taste of Heaven*. He also served as general editor of *The Reformation Study Bible*.

Dr. Sproul and his wife, Vesta, make their home in Longwood, Florida.

℞
Reformation Trust
P U B L I S H I N G

Reformation Trust Publishing was established by Ligonier Ministries in 2006 to produce books that are true to the historic Christian faith and the doctrines recovered during the Protestant Reformation.

Dr. R.C. Sproul, founder and chairman of Ligonier Ministries, has articulated the vision behind the name of this new publishing arm:

"The word *Reformation* defines the theological perspective we're committed to propagating at Ligonier—that recovery of biblical Christianity in the sixteenth century. We want to produce materials that are consistent and faithful to that. *Trust* involves a kind of fidelity and the idea of a legacy. We seek to perpetuate a tradition, but not a tradition of men. The Bible is the divine tradition. Our legacy, our trust, is to be faithful to that tradition."

Believing that an enduring message deserves an

enduring medium, Reformation Trust is committed to publishing books of real value, using high-quality materials and processes. These books will be an investment that will last.

The authors whose names adorn the covers of Reformation Trust titles will be leading evangelical pastors and scholars, men who are adept at rightly handling the Word of God, such as Dr. Sproul, Dr. Steven J. Lawson, Rev. Richard D. Phillips, and others.

We hope you will find that the heritage, the quality, and the authors behind Reformation Trust will make this a publishing imprint you can rely on to strengthen your Christian walk.

LIGONIER MINISTRIES

Renew your Mind.

We're dedicated to helping Christians know what they believe, why they believe it, how to live it, and how to share it.

In order to grow, we need wise instruction from the mind of God about how to think and what we should think about. God calls us to be transformed by His Spirit rather than conformed to the pattern of thinking in this world. And the way of transformation is through the renewing of our minds. It's our goal to proclaim God's holiness, teach His Word with clarity, and see lives changed as we dig deeper into the rich soil of God's truth.

In 1971, as it is today, the world was filled with challenges to biblical faith. Christians who sought to be equipped to answer these challenges had few options short of going to seminary. R.C. Sproul saw the need to offer a bridge of learning for the growing

Christian but in a way that was accessible and practical, and Ligonier Ministries was born.

Our educational mission continues today through our books, monthly magazine, broadcasts, conferences, teaching series, music, and website. The appetite for these materials continues to grow both domestically and internationally. We believe that when the Bible is taught clearly, God is seen in all of His majesty and holiness — hearts are conquered, minds are renewed, communities are transformed.

Our hope is for Ligonier Ministries to become a trusted resource to help stimulate Gospel conviction and courage. We are excited about the future because we serve a great and sovereign God. And we know what we are called to do.

FOR MORE INFORMATION,
PLEASE VISIT WWW.LIGONIER.ORG
OR CALL 800-435-4343.